Be A
Better
Reader

Level A

Seventh Edition

Nila Banton Smith

Globe
Fearon

Upper Saddle River,
New Jersey

Pronunciation Key

Symbol	Key Word	Respelling
a	act	(akt)
ah	star	(stahr)
ai	dare	(dair)
aw	also	(awl soh)
ay	flavor	(flay vər)
e	end	(end)
ee	eat	(eet)
er	learn	(lern)
	sir	(ser)
	fur	(fer)
i	hit	(hit)
eye	idea	(eye dee ə)
y	like	(lyk)
ir	deer	(dir)
	fear	(fir)
oh	open	(oh pen)
oi	foil	(foil)
	boy	(boi)
or	horn	(horn)
ou	out	(out)
	flower	(flou ər)
oo	hoot	(hoot)
	rule	(rool)
yoo	few	(fyoo)
	use	(yooz)

Symbol	Key Word	Respelling
u	book	(buk)
	put	(put)
uh	cup	(kuhp)
ə	a as in along	(ə lawng)
	e as in moment	(moh mənt)
	i as in modify	(mahd ə fy)
	o as in protect	(prə tekt)
	u as in circus	(ser kəs)
ch	chill	(chil)
g	go	(goh)
j	joke	(johk)
	bridge	(brij)
k	kite	(kyt)
	cart	(kahrt)
ng	bring	(bring)
s	sum	(suhm)
	cent	(sent)
sh	sharp	(shahrp)
th	thin	(thin)
z	zebra	(zee brə)
	pose	(pohz)
zh	treasure	(treszh ər)

Be A Better Reader, Level A, Seventh Edition
Nila Banton Smith

Printed in the United States of America
9 10 11 12 13 14 04 03 02 01 00

C12
ISBN 0-8359-1916-1

Acknowledgments
We wish to express our appreciation for permission to use and adapt copyrighted materials.

The dictionary definitions in this book are reprinted with permission of Macmillan General Reference USA, a Division of Simon & Schuster Inc., from WEBSTER'S NEW WORLD DICTIONARY, Basic School Edition. Copyright © 1983 by Simon & Schuster Inc.

Harold Courlander for the play adaptation of "Anansi's Fishing Expedition." From The Cow-Tail Switch and Other West African Stories, by Harold Courlander and George Herzog. Holt, Rinehart and Winston, 1947. Copyright © 1947, 1973 by Harold Courlander and George Herzog. Used by permission of the authors.

Photo Credits
p. 8: Wide World Photos; **p. 18:** W. Gregory Brown/Animals, Animals; **p. 19:** (*left*) E. R. Degginger/Animals, Animals, (*right*) DPI/© John H. Gerard; **p. 51:** David Madison; **p. 95:** The Bettmann Archive; **p. 96:** Lee Snider/Image Works; **p. 97:** M. Siluk/Image Works; **p. 125:** Smithsonian Institution; **p. 130:** Laurence Gould/Animals, Animals; **p. 140:** The Bettmann Archive; **p. 157:** AFZAI/Photo Researchers; **p. 162:** DPI/Leonard Lee Rue III.

Contents

Unit Four Cars

Unit Five Close to the Earth   118

Unit Six Other Countries   148

How to Use *Be A Better Reader*

For more than thirty years, *Be A Better Reader* has helped students improve their reading skills. *Be A Better Reader* teaches the comprehension and study skills that you need to read and enjoy all types of materials—from library books to the different textbooks that you will encounter in school.

To get the most from *Be A Better Reader*, you should know how the lessons are organized. As you read the following explanations, it will be helpful to look at some of the lessons.

In each of the first four lessons of a unit, you will apply an important skill to a reading selection in literature, social studies, science, or mathematics. Each of these lessons includes the following seven sections.

Skill Focus

This section teaches you a specific skill. You should read the Skill Focus carefully, paying special attention to words that are printed in boldface type. The Skill Focus tells you about a skill that you will use when you read the selection.

Word Clues

This section teaches you how to recognize and use different types of context clues. These clues will help you with the meanings of the underlined words in the selection.

Reading a Literature, Social Studies, Science, or Mathematics Selection

This section introduces the selection that you will read and gives you suggestions about what to look for as you read. The suggestions will help you understand the selection.

Selection

The selections in the literature lessons are similar to those in a literature anthology, library book, newspaper, or magazine. The social studies selec-tions are like chapters in a social studies textbook or encyclopedia. They often include maps and tables. The science selections, like a science textbook, include special words in boldface type and sometimes diagrams. The mathematics selections will help you acquire skill in reading mathematics textbooks.

Recalling Facts

Answers to the questions in this section—the first of three activity sections—can be found in the selection. You will sometimes have to reread parts of the selection to do this activity.

Interpreting Facts

The second activity includes questions whose answers are not directly stated in the selection. For these questions, you must combine the information in the selection with what you already know in order to *infer* the answers.

Skill Focus Activity

In the last activity, you will use the skill that you learned in the Skill Focus section at the beginning of the lesson to answer questions about the selection. If you have difficulty completing this activity, reread the Skill Focus section.

The remaining lessons in each unit give you practice with such skills as using a dictionary, an encyclopedia, and other reference materials; using phonics and syllabication aids in recognizing new words; locating and organizing information; and adjusting reading rate. Other reading skills that are necessary in everyday experience are also covered, such as reading a bus schedule and a menu.

Each time that you learn a new skill in *Be A Better Reader*, look for opportunities to use the skill in your other reading at school and at home. Your reading ability will improve the more you practice reading!

Lesson 1

Sequence of Events

Reading a Literature Selection

▶ Background Information

Have you ever dreamed of going around the world? The Robertson family did, and they decided to make their dream a reality.

"Broken Voyage" is a true story about their trip. They set sail from England in a 43-foot sailboat named the *Lucette*. They made their way halfway around the world to the Pacific Ocean. For part of the trip, the Robertsons sailed in a small raft and finally in a rowboat. Look at the map on page 7 to see just how far the Robertson family traveled. In this selection, you will read about a dangerous adventure that the Robertsons had on the Pacific Ocean.

▶ Skill Focus

As you read a story, pay close attention to the **sequence of events**. One way you can keep track of the plot, or sequence of events in a story, is to think about the story as having three parts: a **beginning**, a **middle**, and an **end**. Most stories follow the same plot

sequence. You can think of a story's sequence of events as a mountain. The most exciting part of the story occurs at the top of the peak.

The following questions may help you to identify the three parts.

Beginning
1. What are the people doing when the story begins?
2. What problems do the people have at first?

Middle
3. What is the most exciting event of the story?
4. What happens as a result of this event?

End
5. What is the most serious problem the people face?
6. How do the people solve this problem by the end of the story?

▶ Word Clues

When you read a word that you do not know, look for context clues to help you understand it. Context clues are words near the unknown word that make its meaning clearer. Read the following sentences.

It was thirteen-year-old Neil's turn to wash dishes and clean the galley after breakfast. The boat's kitchen was very small, but it had everything they needed.

If you do not know the meaning of the word *galley*, the word *kitchen* in the next sentence can help you. The words *kitchen* and *galley* are synonyms. A galley is a ship's kitchen.

Look for **synonym** context clues to find the meaning of the three underlined words in the selection.

▶ Strategy Tip

As you read the story, keep track of the sequence of events. Think about which events happened in the beginning, middle, and end of the story. When you finish, you should be able to recall the important events.

Broken Voyage

The first two days of sailing on the Pacific had been stormy. On the third day, the Robertson family was happy to see the sun rise through the clouds. They had bravely battled the waves of the Pacific in their small sailboat, and they needed a rest.

Their 43-foot sailboat was named the *Lucette*. It had carried the Robertsons from their home in England across the Atlantic and into the Pacific on their journey around the world. They had just left the Galapagos Islands off the northwest coast of South America.

During the last six months, they had sailed the *Lucette* through many storms, but they agreed that the last two days were the worst they had seen. As the Robertsons ate breakfast, they talked happily about the day of quiet sailing ahead.

"But now we have work to do," said Mr. Robertson.

It was thirteen-year-old Neil's turn to wash dishes and clean the galley after breakfast. The boat's kitchen was very small, but it had everything they needed. Neil's twin sister Sandy gathered the broken fishing gear to repair it. Douglas, their older brother, was already at the wheel in the cockpit, keeping the *Lucette* on <u>course</u>. It was his responsibility to make sure that they were going in the right direction.

On deck, Mrs. Robertson picked up the rubbish left by the storm. Below, Mr. Robertson checked the *Lucette's* course. He read the <u>charts</u> to make sure they were on course. According to the maps, the Robertsons were 3,000 miles from the islands where they planned to stop next.

In the galley, Neil washed the last pan and put the towel out to dry. He had finished his work for the morning, and now he planned to read a book. As he headed for the cabin, he could hear the water gently slapping against the sides of the boat. It was a comfortable sound. Neil, who had lived all his life on a farm in England, now called this sailboat his home.

He climbed into his bunk and leaned back to enjoy his book. He had just started to read

> "Yes! Get ready to abandon ship!" shouted Mr. Robertson.

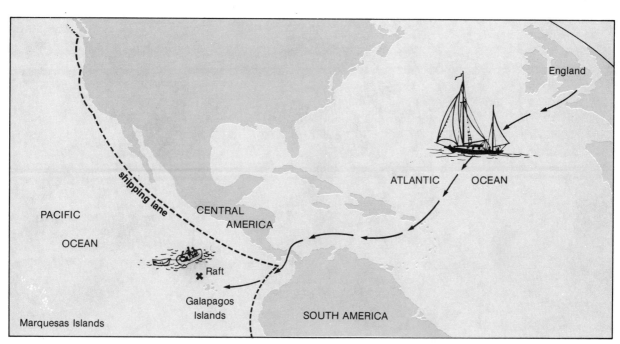

The map shows the course of the Robertson family on the *Lucette* and on the raft.

when something hit the side of the boat. Neil was thrown across the cabin and against the far wall. The *Lucette* was rolling wildly from side to side. Neil was on the floor. His ears were ringing and his shoulder hurt.

As he tried to stand up, Neil heard his family shouting outside. Then he heard his mother yell, "Whales!" A moment later, she ran into the cabin. "Neil, put on your life jacket and get on deck."

The whales had punched a huge hole in the *Lucette's* side, and water was rushing in. As Neil left the cabin, the water already covered the floorboards. He heard his brother Douglas call, "Are we sinking, Dad?"

"Yes! Get ready to abandon ship!" shouted Mr. Robertson. He picked up a knife as he dashed out of the galley. He then cut the ropes to free the small rowboat tied to the mast. "Get the raft ready. We'll need that too," he cried.

The boys pulled down the raft. Douglas pressed the button to fill it with air. Then he and Neil turned to help their father free the rowboat. The sea was nearly up to the *Lucette's* deck. She was sinking fast. The rubber life raft swiftly filled with air. Douglas looked at his father. "When do we lower the raft, Dad?"

"Now! And tie the rowboat to the raft." Mr. Robertson shouted as he ran into the galley.

Water was rolling over the sailboat's decks as Mr. Robertson returned with a bag of food. He had thrown bread, biscuits, sugar, and other foods into the bag. He gave it to Neil. "Put this in the raft and tell everyone to get in. Hurry! She's going under."

Mr. Robertson made one last trip into the galley. He returned with two bags of oranges, lemons, and onions. He tossed them into the rowboat, now tied to the raft. Then he took a last look around. His family waited in the raft. Behind it, the sea stretched as far as he could see. The killer whales were nowhere in sight. The Robertsons were alone. Mr. Robertson jumped into the water and began swimming to the raft. A moment later, the *Lucette* began sinking into the deep, dark heart of the Pacific.

That afternoon, Neil wrote on a piece of sail: *June 15. Neil's log in the lifeboat.* Lucette *sunk by killer whales. Very sad. She went down in 2 minutes.*

The Robertson family aboard the tuna boat that rescued them.

The Robertson family aboard the tuna boat that rescued them.

The Robertsons were lucky to be alive. As the sun went down, they wondered about their chances of staying alive. They had no radio. They were hundreds of miles away from a shipping lane and 3,000 miles from their next port. They would not be missed for at least five weeks.

That night, each person had a piece of biscuit and a sip of water. They divided one orange among them.

A week passed on the lonely Pacific. The rubber life raft had tiny pinholes in the sides. Soon it had to be blown up every hour. High waves forced the Robertsons to bail the raft regularly. After almost three weeks, the family knew that the raft would soon sink. They moved to the tiny rowboat.

The five members of the family crowded together in the little boat. Everyone knew that a sudden movement might cause the boat to tip over. No one moved without warning the others.

Their two greatest problems were thirst and hunger. Their mouths always felt like cotton. Because most of the food from the *Lucette* was gone, they were always hungry. Also, their skin was raw from the burning sun and the stinging salt water.

But as long as the rowboat could carry them, they could stay alive on the dangerous sea. During storms, they caught rain water with a rubber sheet. They filled all the cans they had with water. But each person drank only a little water each day. They did not know when another rain might come. By the time their food was gone, they had learned to catch fish with hooks of wire. Sometimes big turtles poked their heads up next to the boat. Douglas and his father pulled them aboard and quickly slit them open with a knife. The turtle meat would keep them all alive for another day.

The tiny rowboat crept along the course the Robertsons had set for South America. Five weeks had passed since they had abandoned the *Lucette*. "With luck we should make the coast in about three weeks," said Mr. Robertson, "but I'm afraid the wind's changing. So we may have to start rowing . . ."

Suddenly, he stopped talking and stared straight ahead. The others looked at him. "A ship," he said. "There's a ship!"

"Where?" they asked, and everyone turned to look.

"Keep still!" shouted Mr. Robertson. "We don't want to tip over now. I must signal the ship. Neil, hand me a flare from that box."

Carefully standing up, he lit the <u>flare</u> and held it high overhead until it burned his fingers. Then he threw it into the air.

The family watched him, hardly breathing. Mr. Robertson stood frozen, eyes fixed on the distant ship. Moments passed. Then he looked at his family and quietly said, "She's seen us. She's changed course. We're saved."

A passing Japanese tuna boat picked up the Robertsons on July 22. Mr. Robertson was the last to climb on board. He was surprised to see that his family was lying down on the deck. Suddenly, he realized why. Living for 38 days on a raft and in a rowboat had weakened his legs, too. Four days later, the Robertson family was back on land.

RECALLING FACTS

Write the answers to the following questions on the lines provided. If necessary, you may go back to the selection to find an answer.

1. Who are the members of the Robertson family?

_____

_____

_____

_____

2. What course did the Robertsons sail?

_____

_____

_____

3. At what point in the Robertson's journey does this story begin?

_____

_____

4. Tell what work each member of the Robertson family had to do after breakfast.

Mrs. Robertson _____

Mr. Robertson _____

_____

Sandy _____

Neil _____

Douglas _____

5. What did Neil do after he finished cleaning the galley?

_____

6. What caused the *Lucette* to sink?

_____

_____

7. What are the two most serious problems that the Robertsons faced at sea?

_____

_____

8. How did the Robertsons get fresh drinking water?

_____

_____

9. How did they get food?

_____

10. Why did Mr. Robertson tell the family to keep still when he saw a ship?

_____

11. What effect did living at sea for 38 days have on the Robertsons?

_____

_____

12. Write the letter of the correct meaning in front of each word.

_____ course   a. maps used by sailors

_____ charts   b. the direction taken by a ship

_____ flare   c. a bright light used to signal for help

INTERPRETING FACTS

Not all questions about a story are answered directly in the story. For the following questions, you will have to figure out answers not directly stated in the story. Write the answers to the questions on the lines provided.

1. At what time of day did the *Lucette* sink? How do you know?

_____

_____

_____

2. Why did the Robertsons take the rowboat with them?

_____

_____

_____

_____

3. Why did the Robertsons use the raft instead of the rowboat?

_____

_____

4. Put a check mark before the words that describe the Robertson family.

_____ playful   _____ lazy

_____ responsible   _____ cooperative

_____ helpful   _____ nervous

5. What is the meaning of the title "Broken Voyage"?

_____

_____

_____

_____

SKILL FOCUS

Below are some of the events in "Broken Voyage." On the numbered lines, write the events in the sequence in which they took place. Which events happened at the beginning of the story? in the middle? at the end? Then on the blank lines, fill in a different incident that occurs during each part of the story.

    a. Killer whales hit the _Lucette_.

    b. The Robertsons are alone with little food and water.

    c. The Robertsons get into the rubber raft and watch the _Lucette_ sink.

    d. A passing ship rescues the Robertsons.

    e. The Robertsons hit storms in the Pacific.

    f. The Robertsons look forward to a quiet day of sailing.

Beginning

1. _____

2. _____

   _____

Middle

3. _____

4. _____

   _____

End

5. _____

6. _____

   _____

▶ **Real Life Connections** Imagine being on board the _Lucette_ as it starts to sink. What is the first thing that you might do to help the situation?

Cause and Effect

Reading a Social Studies Selection

▶ Background Information

Whales have been hunted for many centuries and in many parts of the world. As a result of their being hunted, many types of whales are extinct. These whales no longer exist. Other types of whales are endangered. There are so few of these types of whales that if they are not protected, they may soon become extinct. Laws in the United States now prohibit people from hunting certain types of whales. However, some countries around the world still allow people to hunt them.

As you read "The Whaling Industry," you will find out when the whaling industry started and what caused it to grow. You will also find out about the two kinds of whales that whalers hunted most often. After reading the selection, you will know what caused the end of the American whaling industry.

When reading textbooks, you may find words that are difficult to say, or pronounce. Sometimes these words are *respelled* to help you pronounce them. Sometimes

the meaning of the word is explained in a *definition*. In this selection, the first word that is respelled is *baleen* (bə LEEN). As you read, look for other words that are respelled. Try saying each word quietly to yourself.

▶ Skill Focus

Many events that you read about in textbooks are connected by **cause and effect**. When events are connected in this way, it means one event or condition (the cause) made another event happen (the effect). Look at the following example.

Cause: People needed food and oil.

Effect: They hunted whales for food and oil.

Because people needed food and oil, they hunted whales. The cause and effect are connected.

When you read this article, try to find the conditions and events that are connected in this way. When you come to an important event, think about what caused it to happen.

▶ Word Clues

Read the sentences below. Look for context clues that explain the underlined word.

> By 1700, whales had become very important for their underlined{blubber}, whalebone, and meat. Blubber is the fat under the skin of the whale.

If you do not know the meaning of the word *blubber* in the first sentence, read on. The second sentence states what the word *blubber* means. A word meaning that is stated directly can often be found before or after a new word.

Use **definition** context clues to find the meaning of the three underlined words in the selection.

▶ Strategy Tip

Before you read "The Whaling Industry," look at the headings in heavy type. Look at the pictures and read their captions. As you read the article, remember to look for the important events and what caused them.

The Whaling Industry

People have hunted whales for food and oil since early times. Even before there were whaling voyages, people killed whales that they found washed up on beaches. Later, people used boats to hunt whales. They killed whales with hand-thrown <u>harpoons</u>. A harpoon is a spear with a line attached to it. Today many countries are against commercial whaling.

The Early Days of Whaling

The people of southern France and northern Spain hunted whales during the 1200s. They made the first whaling voyages. They used large ships in the part of the Atlantic Ocean called the Bay of Biscay. Each ship carried small boats in which whalers set out to kill whales. When whales no longer came close to shore, the whalers went farther out to sea. During the 1500s, they hunted whales across the Atlantic Ocean as far as Newfoundland.

In the 1600s, Dutch and English sailors found many whales in the Arctic waters. Soon a group of islands north of Norway became the center of Arctic whaling.

At the same time, American Indians were also hunting whales. They hunted whales in much the same way as the first whalers. Shortly after the American colonists arrived in the 1600s, they hunted whales off the Atlantic coast. Lookout towers were built in many New England towns along the coast. When whales were sighted from the towers, the whalers launched their boats.

The "Right" Whale to Hunt

The whales that were hunted up to this time had no teeth. They are called baleen (bə LEEN) whales.

Baleen whales have whalebone, or baleen, instead of teeth. They have about four hundred thin plates of baleen in their mouths. Through these plates, baleen whales filter sea water to strain out the small fish they feed on.

There are many kinds of baleen whales. The whalers, however, hunted for the kind that swam slowly, was easily overtaken, floated when dead, and provided great quantities of oil and whalebone. Because this whale was the right kind to hunt, whalers called it the right whale. Today the whale is still called by that name.

By 1700, whales had become very important for their blubber, whalebone, and meat. Blubber is the fat under the skin of the whale. Nearly two hundred gallons of whale oil could be gotten from one ton of melted blubber. This oil was used for cooking and lighting lamps. Whalebone was used for fishing rods, buggy whips, and umbrellas. Whale meat was cooked and eaten.

Discovery of the Sperm Whale

In 1712, an American whaling ship was caught in a storm at sea and blown off course. The whalers came upon a school of whales, killed one, and brought it back to shore. To the whalers' surprise, the whale, unlike a right whale, had teeth.

Whales with teeth are called toothed whales. The New England whalers had discovered the largest of the toothed whales, the sperm whale. The sperm whale was larger and stronger than the right whale. This discovery started the American whaling industry.

The Golden Age of American Whaling

✔ The sperm whale soon became the prime catch of the American whalers. By 1800, Americans were hunting sperm whales throughout the Atlantic Ocean. The town of New Bedford in Massachusetts became the whaling capital of the world. Nantucket, Salem, and other New England cities with harbors also became centers for large whaling fleets. By 1835, Americans were whaling in the Pacific Ocean. San Francisco became an important whaling center.

✔ Whalers got three valuable substances from sperm whales. The first was sperm oil, which was used for lamps. It was better than the oil of the right whale. Another important substance was <u>spermaceti</u> (sper mə SET ee). Spermaceti is a pure wax found in the whale's head. It was used in making candles. A third substance, called <u>ambergris</u> (am ber GREES), was used for perfumes. The high value of sperm oil, spermaceti, and ambergris more than made up for the absence of whalebone in the sperm whale.

Baleen hangs from the upper jaw of baleen whales.

Teeth grow from the lower jaw of most toothed whales.

The Decline of the Whaling Industry

The American sperm whaling industry grew until about 1850. Whale oil had become the chief lamp fuel. However, when gold was found in 1848, many whalers left their ships to search for gold in California. During the Civil War, the Confederate navy sunk many whaling ships. With fewer whalers and ships, whaling began to suffer. The discovery of oil in the ground hurt whaling most of all. It led to the start of a new industry. Soon it was cheaper to use this oil for lamps than to use sperm oil.

> Whales spend most of their life on the surface of the water and are able to swim up to 35 miles per hour.

Whaling in the Twentieth Century

During the first half of the 1900s, whaling fleets killed large numbers of whales. As a result, they reduced the world's whale population and endangered many kinds of whales. Nevertheless, whale oil and sperm oil are still used in making cosmetics and soaps. Ambergris is still used in making perfumes, Whalebone is often ground up and used as meal for livestock. People in Japan and Norway, still eat the meat of baleen whales.

To prevent the extinction of certain whales, several nations met in 1946 and formed the International Whaling Commission. This commission decides the length of the whaling season, limits the number of whales that may be killed each year, and does not allow the killing of certain whales. Because the whale population continued to decline, the commission placed a ban on commercial whaling, which was supported by twenty-five nations and began in 1986. Other antiwhaling groups have since tried to limit further or to ban whaling altogether.

RECALLING FACTS

Write the answers to the following questions on the lines provided. You may go back to the selection to find an answer. Use the headings in the selection to help you find information.

1. Who were the first whalers?

_____

_____

2. What is baleen?

_____

_____

3. Why did the early whalers hunt for the right whale?

_____

_____

_____

4. Name the two groups of whales.

_____

_____

5. What discovery caused the beginning of the whaling industry in America?

_____

_____

6. Name one difference between right whales and sperm whales.

_____

_____

7. What parts of the right whale were valuable?

_____

_____

8. What parts of the sperm whale were valuable?

_____

_____

9. Tell one event that caused the decline of whaling in America.

_____

_____

_____

10. Number the following events in the order in which they happened.

_____ The islands north of Norway became the center of Arctic whaling.

_____ The discovery of ground oil hurt the whaling industry.

_____ Whalers hunted whales in the Bay of Biscay.

_____ New Bedford, Massachusetts, became the whaling capital of the world.

_____ Twenty-five nations supported a ban on commercial whaling.

11. Two paragraphs have check marks next to them. Reread both paragraphs. Then underline the sentence that tells what each paragraph is about.

12. Write the letter of the correct meaning in front of each word.

_____ harpoons   **a.** a pure wax found in the head of sperm whales

_____ spermaceti   **b.** spears used to kill whales

_____ ambergris   **c.** a substance found in sperm whales that is used in making perfume

---

INTERPRETING FACTS

Not all questions about a selection are answered directly in the selection. For the following questions, you will have to figure out answers not directly stated in the selection. Write the answers to the questions on the lines provided.

1. Why was the sperm whale more valuable than the right whale?

_____

_____

_____

_____

_____

_____

2. Why was the discovery of ground oil one of the major causes of the decline of whaling in America?

_____

_____

_____

_____

_____

_____

3. Do you think whaling should be outlawed? Write a paragraph using facts from the selection to support your opinion.

_____

_____

_____

_____

SKILL FOCUS

Match each cause with its effect. You may need to reread the selection.

Cause	Effect
1. _____ Because whales no longer used the Bay of Biscay as a feeding ground,	**a.** whales became very important.
2. _____ Because the Dutch and English found Arctic waters filled with whales,	**b.** the sperm whale became the prize catch of American whalers.
3. _____ Because whale meat, blubber, and whalebone were valuable,	**c.** a ban was placed on commercial whaling.
4. _____ Because American whalers were hunting whales throughout the Atlantic,	**d.** whale oil became the chief source of lamp fuel.
5. _____ Because whalers were able to get valuable sperm oil, spermaceti, and ambergris from sperm whales,	**e.** the first whalers went farther out to sea.
6. _____ Because there was an abundance of whale oil,	**f.** the whaling industry in the United States rapidly declined.
7. _____ As a result of the California Gold Rush, the Civil War, and the discovery of oil,	**g.** many New England cities became whaling centers.
8. _____ As a result of whaling fleets' killing large numbers of whales in the early 1900s,	**h.** the islands north of Norway became the center of Arctic whaling.
9. _____ Because the number of whales declined,	**i.** there is a smaller whale population today.

▶ **Real Life Connections** Do you think that whaling should be outlawed in all parts of the world? Tell why or why not.

Lesson 3

Classifying

Reading a Science Selection

► Background Information

The ocean covers more than 70 percent of the earth's surface. However, until recently the ocean has been largely a mystery to us. Oceanography–the study of the ocean–has come a long way since it started thousands of years ago.

In ancient Greece, the ocean was a subject of great interest. The Greeks did not have the instruments available to unlock many of the secrets of the ocean. Since then, people have been studying the ocean. In the 1800s, exploration of the ocean reached new heights. S.C.U.B.A. gear, underwater breathing equipment, and underwater laboratories have made the study of the ocean easier. People now have the ability to explore all but the deepest bottoms of the ocean. There are hopes that this exploration will lead to discoveries that may help better humankind.

While there are still many mysteries of the deep, many discoveries have been made. The ocean is rich with many kinds of life. Many varieties of plants and animals live beneath the surface of the ocean. Of course, these differences (and similarities) are what allows scientists to classify these animals. Aquatic animals are classified into three different groups, which you will read about in this selection.

► Skill Focus

Sometimes information is organized by **classifying** similar objects or ideas into groups. It is then easier to see similarities and differences among these groups. Classifying is very helpful for people who work with a great number of objects, as scientists often do.

When scientists classify plants and animals, they take large groups and break them up into smaller groups. The members of each smaller group are similar in some way. Goldfish and sharks are similar—they are both in the group called *fish*. Clams live in the water, but they belong to a different group than goldfish and sharks. Lobsters and crabs live in the water like fish, but they belong to yet another group.

When reading about groups, notice the important details. Ask yourself questions like the following.

1. What is similar about the animals that scientists put in the same group?
2. How are the animals in one group different from the animals in another group?

► Word Clues

Pictures can be used as context clues. Sometimes pictures help you with the meaning of a word. Look at Figure 1 on page 18. The picture helps you understand the meaning of the word *haddock*.

Use pictures to find the meaning of the two underlined words in the selection.

► **Strategy Tip**

When reading a science selection, it is helpful to look at the words that are printed in heavy, or **boldface**, type. These words are the most important in the selection. Look at the three headings in the selection. Each heading tells you the name of a group of ocean animals.

Three Groups of Water Animals

The Group Called Fish

Haddock, codfish, and mackerel are all fish. The body of a fish has a backbone and a skeleton. Animals that have backbones are known as **vertebrates** (VER tə brats). The bodies of most fish are covered with flat scales, like shingles on a roof. Fish can breathe underwater through gills. Most fish also have air bladders inside their bodies. These air bladders are filled with gases. By changing the amount of gas in its air bladder, a fish can move up or down through the water.

A fish uses its tail to push itself through the water. The shape of its body helps it move through the water easily. Most fish have fins that they use for balancing, steering, and braking.

Sharks are fish, but they do not have true backbones or air bladders. Some sharks are dangerous to people. The great white shark can be as much as 7.6 meters long. White sharks have attacked swimmers as far north as Cape Cod on the Atlantic coast. Other dangerous sharks are the hammerhead shark and the tiger shark.

Fish are a very important food for people. Hundreds of millions of dollars' worth of fish are sold every year. Scientists are helping to feed the people of the world by finding new ways to raise fish.

Figure 1. The rock cod above, along with haddock and mackerel, belongs to the group called fish.

The Group Called Mollusks

Oysters, scallops, clams, snails, squids, and octopuses are all **mollusks** (MAH lusks). The word *mollusk* means "soft-bodied." All mollusks have soft bodies. Many have tough, hard shells for protection. Clams, oysters, and scallops have two-piece shells that are connected by a hinge of muscle. Their soft, fleshy bodies are used as food by many people.

Mollusks have no backbones, but they do have gills. Mollusks are sometimes called shellfish, but they are not really fish.

For protection, the squid depends not on a heavy shell, but on its ability to swim quickly. The octopus does not have a shell either. It can also move quickly. The octopus has eight arms, and the squid has ten arms.

You may have heard "sea-monster" stories of giant squids and octopuses. However, most squids and octopuses are not giants. They swim away when they see a large creature. They can also squirt a black fluid that forms a dark cloud in the water. This makes it more difficult for their enemies to find them.

Scallops move through the water in an interesting way. These mollusks "clap" their two shells together. The large muscle that closes the scallop shell is enjoyed as a food by many people. The rest of the body is thrown away.

Oysters are a very good food. Some oysters grow pearls inside their shells. In Japan people make oysters grow pearls by placing single grains of sand inside the oysters' shells. The pearls grow around these grains of sand. After several years, the oysters produce a very valuable crop of pearls.

The Group Called Crustaceans

Another group of animals that live mostly in salt water is called the **crustaceans** (krus TA shənz). Crustaceans are covered with a heavy crust or hard shell. They have gills for breathing underwater. Their bodies have many joints and sections but no backbones. Most of them move by crawling. <u>Lobsters</u>, crabs, and shrimp are all crustaceans.

Lobsters are caught in wooden or metal traps called lobster pots. When alive, lobsters are a greenish-blue color. When they are cooked, their shells turn a bright red.

Many kinds of crabs are found along the seashore. Among these are the blue crab, the rock crab, the hermit crab, and the fiddler crab. Crabs that have shed their hard shells are called soft-shelled crabs. The soft-shelled blue crab is used for food.

Shrimps found in salt water have narrower bodies than crabs. Like lobsters and crabs, shrimps are valued as a food. Every year, large numbers of shrimps and other crustaceans are sold frozen or canned at stores or fresh at fish markets.

Figure 2. The giant clam belongs to the group called mollusks.

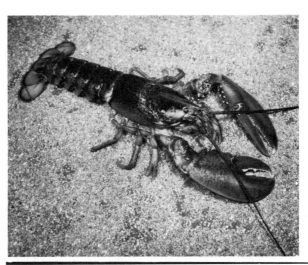

Figure 3. The lobster belongs to the group called crustaceans.

RECALLING FACTS

Write the answers to the following questions on the lines provided. You may go back to the selection to find an answer.

1. Name three kinds of fish.

_____

2. How does a fish use its tail?

_____

_____

3. How does the shape of a fish help it?

_____

_____

4. Name three ways in which a fish uses its fins.

_____

_____

5. What is one way a fish moves up through the water?

_____

_____

6. Octopuses can squirt a black fluid. What effect does the fluid have on their enemies?

_____

_____

7. What do clams and oysters have that protect them from their enemies?

_____

8. Do mollusks have backbones?

_____

9. How do people make oysters grow pearls?

_____

_____

_____

10. What word can you find in the word *crustacean* that helps you to remember something important about these animals?

_____

_____

11. Do crustaceans have backbones?

_____

_____

12. Name four kinds of crabs.

_____

_____

13. How is a soft-shelled crab different from a hard-shelled crab?

_____

_____

14. How do these creatures move?
    a. fish

_____

_____

    b. scallops

_____

_____

    c. most crustaceans

_____

_____

15. What does the squid rely on to protect itself?

_____

_____

16. Write the letter of the correct definition on the line in front of each word.

____ lobster   a. an animal covered by a hard shell

____ scallop   b. an animal with two claws and many legs

INTERPRETING FACTS

Not all questions about a selection are answered directly in the selection. For the following questions, you will have to figure out answers not directly stated in the selection. In questions 1 and 2, circle the letter of the best answer.

1. What would be the effect of more gas in a fish's air bladder?
   a. The fish would move up.
   b. The fish would move down.

2. Why would an oyster form a pearl around a grain of sand?
   a. The sand chills it.
   b. The sand irritates it.
   c. The sand makes it hungry.

3. Why might a shark sink when it stops swimming?

_____

_____

Write answers to the questions in the following table. The first one has been started for you.

	What are their bodies like?	What covers their bodies?
Fish	Fish have backbones and skeletons. _____	_____ _____ _____
Mollusks	_____ _____ _____	_____ _____ _____
Crustaceans	_____ _____ _____	_____ _____ _____

Oysters, snails, crabs, codfish, clams, lobsters, mackerel, scallops, haddock, and shrimps are all water animals. Write the name of each animal under the heading where it belongs.

Fish	*Mollusks*	*Crustaceans*
_____	_____	_____
_____	_____	_____
_____	_____	_____
_____	_____	_____

▶ **Real Life Connections** Work with a partner to research the following question: Why are fish an important food for the world?

Word Problems

Reading a Mathematics Selection

▶ Background Information

You might wonder why you have to learn how to do word problems. You've probably said to yourself, "I'll never ever need to know that!" Sometimes you may even be right.

However, sometimes the skills that you learn at school can be used each and every day of your life. Being able to do word problems is one of these skills that you will definitely need to know.

For example, let's say that your mother gives you $10 to go to the grocery store to buy a quart of milk ($.99), a dozen eggs ($1.29), and a pint of ice cream ($3.49). You may not know it, but this is a word problem.

What if this example were changed around to look like this?

A quart of milk costs $.99. A dozen eggs costs $1.29. A pint of ice cream costs $3.49. Greg's mother asks him to buy these three items at the grocery store. What will Greg's change be if his mother gives him $10? 20?

You see, everyone uses word problems. Doctors use them to diagnose patients. Police officers use them to solve crimes. Scientists use them to learn about ocean animals, plants and rocks. In "Solving Word Problems," you will read about a five-step process for solving word problems.

▶ Skill Focus

There are five steps you should follow in solving a word problem.

First, read the problem. Be sure that you are familiar with all the words, especially the labels that are used with each number. For example, meters, dollars, and kilometers are some commonly used labels. Think about what question is being asked. Try to picture the information that is given. Read the problem again to be sure that you understand it.

Second, decide how to find the answer. It may be helpful to draw a picture of the information that is given. Should you add, subtract, multiply, or divide? Look for key words in the last sentence.

Third, estimate the answer. Use rounded numbers to make an estimate.

Fourth, carry out the plan. Do the arithmetic that will give you the answer.

Fifth, reread the problem. Is the answer logical? How close is it to your estimate?

Be sure that your answer includes the correct label(s). Without the correct labels, your answer is incomplete.

▶ Word Clues

Certain words can give you a clue to how to find the answer in a word problem. For example, words, such as *in all, total, together,* and *sum,* often show that you have to combine groups, or add, to find the answer. Words, such as *difference, more, shorter, longer, less, left, change,* and *part,* often show that you have to compare, or subtract, to find the answer. Look for these word clues in the last sentence of a problem.

▶ Strategy Tip

Scientists use numbers in word problems to learn about ocean animals, plants, and rocks. In this selection, you will learn how to use five steps in solving word problems.

Solving Word Problems

Scientists have learned a great deal about the ocean by measuring and counting the things found there. Knowing how to work with different number facts can help you answer questions. Suppose these two facts about whales are known.

A humpback whale is 18 meters long.

A blue whale is 31 meters long.

One question that can be asked is "What is the difference in length between the blue whale and the humpback whale?" How can the facts be used to answer this question? Follow the five steps below.

READ THE PROBLEM

A humpback whale is 18 meters long. A blue whale is 31 meters long. What is the difference in length between the blue whale and the humpback whale?

Read the problem again. Be sure that you know the label that is used with each number fact. Are there any words that you do not know? If so, look them up to find their meanings. What question does the problem ask? Often the question is asked in the last sentence: *What is the difference in length between the blue whale and the humpback whale?*

DECIDE HOW TO FIND THE ANSWER

It is helpful to make a drawing or diagram.

31 Meters
———————— Blue Whale
18 Meters
——— Humpback Whale

Should the numbers be added, subtracted, multiplied, or divided to answer the question? *They should be subtracted because you are comparing lengths.* The key word *difference* tells you that you need to subtract.

ESTIMATE THE ANSWER

Use rounded numbers to help make an estimate. Round to the nearest ten and then subtract.

$$30 - 20 = 10$$

Your estimate is 10.

CARRY OUT THE PLAN

Do the arithmetic.

$$31 - 18 = 13$$

REREAD THE PROBLEM

After rereading the problem, write the complete answer.

The blue whale is 13 meters longer.

Does the answer make sense? How close is your answer to your estimate? If the answer is not close to your estimate, you should start all over.

These five steps can be used to help solve all word problems.

1. Read the problem.
2. Decide how to find the answer.
3. Estimate the answer.
4. Carry out the plan.
5. Reread the problem.

Read: Mt. Pico is 6,100 meters from the ocean bottom to sea level. Then it rises 2,300 meters above the sea. What is the total height of Mt. Pico?

Decide:

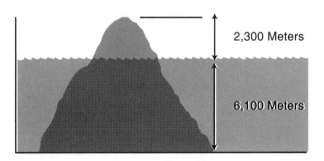

2,300 Meters

6,100 Meters

To find the answer to this problem, you need to combine the two number facts. The word *total* is a clue to use addition. Add the numbers to put the two measurements together.

Estimate: Round each number to the nearest thousand and add.

$$2,000 + 6,000 = 8,000.$$

Carry Out: $2,300 + 6,100 = 8,400$

Reread: After reading the problem, write the complete answer: Mt. Pico is 8,400 meters tall. Does this answer make sense? How close is this answer to your estimate?

RECALLING FACTS

Write the answers to the following questions on the lines provided.

1. What label is used in the example problem on page 23?

   _____

   _____

2. What should you do if your answer is quite different from your estimate?

   _____

   _____

3. Write the five steps for solving word problems.

   a. _____

   b. _____

   c. _____

   d. _____

   e. _____

4. What technique does the selection suggest for finding the answer to a word problem.

   _____

INTERPRETING FACTS

Not all questions about a selection are answered directly in the selection. For the following questions, you will have to figure out answers not directly stated in the selection. Write the answers to the questions on the lines provided.

1. Why is making an estimate important in problem solving?

   _____

   _____

2. If your estimate is 100 and your answer is 104, why might your answer be correct?

   _____

   _____

3. If your estimate is 4 and your answer is 8, why might your answer be incorrect?

   _____

   _____

SKILL FOCUS

Use the five steps to solve these word problems. The first one is started for you. If necessary, draw pictures or diagrams on another sheet of paper to help you with the second step.

1. Read: In May a tuna weighs 181 kilograms. By September it has gained 136 kilograms. What is the tuna's total weight in September?

   Decide: Add to put the two weights together. _____

   Estimate: _____

   Carry Out: _____

   Reread: _____

2. Read: Most deep sea divers can go only 40 meters under water. Some divers can go 21 meters deeper. How deep can the best divers go?

   Decide: _____

   Estimate: _____

   Carry Out: _____

   Reread: _____

3. Read: A blue marlin swims 48 kilometers per hour. A dolphin swims 40 kilometers per hour. What is the difference between the two speeds?

   Decide: _____

   Estimate: _____

   Carry Out: _____

   Reread: _____

4. Read: The highest ocean mountain is 9,693 meters tall. The highest land mountain is 8,840 meters. How much lower is the land mountain?

   Decide: _____

   Estimate: _____

   Carry Out: _____

   Reread: _____

5. Read: The Pacific Ocean covers 166,000,000 square kilometers, the Atlantic Ocean covers 87,000,000 square kilometers, and the Indian Ocean covers 73,000,000 square kilometers. What is their area all together?

   Decide: _____

   Estimate: _____

   Carry Out: _____

   Reread: _____

6. Read: The Java Trench is 7,125 meters deep. The Mariana Trench is 10,924 meters deep. How much deeper is the Mariana Trench?

   Decide: _____

   Estimate: _____

   Carry Out: _____

   Reread: _____

▶ **Real Life Connections** Estimate the number of students in your school. Then find out the exact number. What's the difference? How close was your estimate?

Consonants

Say each picture name. Listen to the beginning sound. On the line, write the letter that stands for the **consonant** sound you hear at the beginning of the picture name.

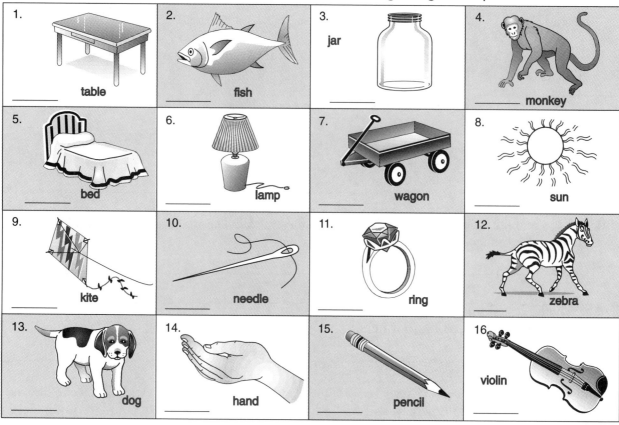

1. table
2. fish
3. jar
4. monkey
5. bed
6. lamp
7. wagon
8. sun
9. kite
10. needle
11. ring
12. zebra
13. dog
14. hand
15. pencil
16. violin

Say each picture name. Listen to the ending sound. On the line, write the letter that stands for the **consonant** sound you hear at the end of the picture name.

1. crab
2. door
3. bed
4. nail
5. book
6. train
7. soap
8. drum
9. foot
10. horse
11. log
12. muff

Main Idea

In many of the paragraphs that you read, one sentence is more important than the others. This sentence states the main idea of the paragraph. The main idea is the idea that is most important in the paragraph. It tells what the paragraph is about. Finding the sentence with the main idea will be helpful to you in all your studies.

Read the following paragraphs. Below each one are three sentences from the paragraph. Underline the sentence that is the main idea of the paragraph.

Oysters

1. The largest supply of oysters in the world is found in Atlantic waters. Oysters live in quiet, shallow waters. They like bays and river mouths. The Atlantic coast has quiet bays. This is why so many more oysters are found along this coast than in any other waters.

    a. Oysters live in quiet, shallow waters.
    b. The Atlantic coast has quiet bays.
    c. The largest supply of oysters in the world is found in Atlantic waters.

2. Oysters like warm waters. They grow best in temperatures between 66°F and 70°F. In southern waters they grow to full size in two to three years. In the north, it takes about four years for them to grow.

    a. Oysters like warm waters.
    b. In southern waters they grow to full size in two to three years.
    c. In the north, it takes about four years for them to grow.

3. Oysters are grown as a crop. The people who make oyster farms set up the beds where the bottom is hard mud. They clean the rubbish from the beds. Then they place seed oysters in the beds. They feed and care for the oysters until the crop is ready to harvest.

    a. They clean the rubbish from the beds.
    b. Oysters are grown as a crop.
    c. Then they place seed oysters in the beds.

4. Fine pearls come from "pearl oysters." Once in a while, a pearl is found in an edible oyster, but it is a low-grade pearl. Pearl oysters grow in the warm waters of southern seas.

    a. Once in a while, a pearl is found in an edible oyster, but it is a low-grade pearl.
    b. Pearl oysters grow in the warm waters of southern seas.
    c. Fine pearls come from "pearl oysters."

5. Oysters have many enemies. Boring snails bore a hole through oysters' shells and eat the oysters. Crabs attack small and weak oysters and kill them. Fish with sharp teeth crush and eat young oysters.

    a. Crabs attack small and weak oysters and kill them.
    b. Oysters have many enemies.
    c. Fish with sharp teeth crush and eat young oysters.

6. Oysters have been valuable to people for hundreds of years. Early people prized beautiful pearls for jewelry. They considered oysters to be an important source of food.

    a. Early people prized beautiful pearls for jewelry.
    b. Oysters have been valuable to people for hundreds of years.
    c. They considered oysters to be an important source of food.

Which sentence in each paragraph has the main idea? _____

Following Directions

Flight attendants on airplanes show passengers how to use safety and emergency devices, such as seat belts and oxygen masks. If the plane is flying over an ocean or other large body of water, the flight attendants also show how to use life jackets. Cards with directions and drawings for using life jackets are in the seat packets for each passenger to read.

Below are the steps for using a life jacket. Each step is numbered and illustrated. The directions are given in English and Spanish. Study the directions carefully, as well as the illustrations, so that you will understand how a life jacket works.

1 Life Jackets Under Seats
Chalecos Salvavidas Baja el Asiento

2 Pull Tab and Remove Jacket from Package
Tire de la Cinta y Remueva el Chaleco

3 Put Jacket over Head
Ponga el Chaleco Sobre la Cabeza

4 Hook Back of Jacket to Front
Una la Parte de Atras del Chaleco a la Parte Delantera

A. Below, in the incorrect order, are the steps to follow when using a life jacket. Write 1 in front of the step to follow first, 2 in front of the step to follow next, and so on.

_____ Put the life jacket on over your head, keeping the tabs in front.

_____ Tighten the belt around your waist by pulling the ends of the belt.

_____ If the life jacket does not fill up with air, blow into the tubes to inflate it.

_____ Get the package containing the life jacket from under your seat.

_____ After leaving the plane, pull down on the tabs to inflate the life jacket.

_____ Buckle both ends of the belt to the center ring on the front of the life jacket.

_____ If it is dark outside, pull down on the center tab for light.

_____ Pull the tab to open the package and remove the life jacket.

B. Choose one of the topics listed below and write directions for it. Make sure that your directions are clear enough for other students to follow them.

1. how to play your favorite game

2. how to make your favorite sandwich or dessert

3. how to build a model car, airplane, or boat

4. how to use your personal computer

_____

_____

_____

_____

_____

5 Tighten Around Waist
Ajusta la Correa por el Cinturon

6 After Leaving Aircraft, Pull Tabs to Inflate
Despues de Salir del Avion, Tire de las Cintas Para Inflar

7 Oral Inflation Tubes
Tubos Para Inflar con la Boca

8 If Dark, Pull Center Tab to Activate Light
Si esta Obscura, Tire de la Cinta del Centro Para Activar la Linterna

Consonant Blends

Many words begin with the sound of just one consonant. Some words have two consonants at the beginning. If you hear the consonant sounds that both letters stand for, the two letters are called a **consonant blend**. The following are called *r* blends.

br   cr   dr   fr   gr   pr   tr

Say each picture name. Listen to the beginning sounds. On the line, write the blend listed above that stands for the consonant sounds that you hear at the beginning of the picture name.

Consonant Blends

A **consonant blend** is two or more consonant letters that blend together in such a way that the consonant sound each stands for is heard. Here are some *l* blends.

bl   cl   fl   gl   pl   sl

Say each picture name. Listen to the beginning sounds. On the line, write the blend listed above that stands for the consonant sounds that you hear at the beginning of the picture name.

1. _____ plate

2. claw _____

3. glass _____

4. fly _____

5. blocks _____

6. glove _____

7. slide _____

8. clown _____

9. flag _____

10. _____ blanket

11. clam _____

12. flowers _____

13. slippers _____

14. globe _____

15. _____ blimp

16. plow _____

17. clock _____

18. blade _____

19. _____ glasses

20. plug _____

21. _____ pliers

22. sleep _____

23. _____ playpen

24. blouse _____

25. flame _____

26. clip _____

27. _____ sled

28. glue _____

29. slice _____

30. blow _____

31. _____ plus

32. glass _____

Lesson 10

Consonant Blends

Some words have two consonants at the beginning of them. If you hear the sounds that both of these letters stand for, the two letters are called a **consonant blend**. Here are some *s* blends.

sc   sm   sn   sp   st   sw

Say each picture name. Listen to the beginning sounds. On the line, write the blend listed above that stands for the consonant sounds that you hear at the beginning of the picture name.

1. star
2. swan
3. snail
4. spool
5. smoke
6. scale
7. spider
8. snake
9. scarecrow
10. swing
11. smile
12. stool
13. sweater
14. sneaker
15. spoon
16. scarf
17. stamp
18. smell
19. stove
20. switch
21. smock
22. scout
23. snowflake
24. spear
25. sneeze
26. stairs
27. sweep
28. spaceship
29. stapler
30. snorkel
31. swim
32. spaghetti

Lesson 11

Long and Short Vowel Sounds

Say the word *apple*. Listen to its beginning sound. The sound you hear at the beginning of the word *apple* is called the short sound of *a*. Other **short vowel sounds** are *e* as in *egg*, *i* as in *it*, *o* as in *on*, and *u* as in *umbrella*. Most dictionaries do not mark short vowel sounds.

Long vowel sounds give the name of the vowel, as *a* in *age*, *e* in *eagle*, *i* in *ice*, *o* in *open*, and *u* in *unit*. Most dictionaries mark long vowel sounds with a macron (‾) above the vowel letter. Example: āge.

Words Ending in *e*

Look at each picture. Read the words. Write the word that names the picture.

pin or pine?	rob or robe?	cub or cube?	can or cane?
_____	_____	_____	_____

Write a one-word answer to each question in the headings. Then complete Guide 1.

	Is the first vowel sound long or short?	*Is there an e at the end of the word?*	*Is the e silent or sounded?*
1. page	_____	_____	_____
2. ice	_____	_____	_____
3. globe	_____	_____	_____

> **Guide 1:** When a word contains two vowels, one of which is final _____, the first vowel is usually _____, and the final *e* is _____.

Words That Do Not End in *e*

Write a one-word answer to each question in the headings. Then complete Guide 2.

	Is the first vowel sound long or short?	*Is there a vowel at the end of the word?*
1. sand	_____	_____
2. bend	_____	_____
3. rock	_____	_____

> **Guide 2:** When a word contains only one vowel, and that vowel is not at the end of the word, the _____ is usually _____.

Long and Short Vowel Sounds

The two guides that you have learned to help you decide whether the vowel sound in a one-syllable word is long or short are given below with a word missing in each one. Write a word on the line to complete each guide.

Guide 1: When a word contains two vowels, one of which is final *e*, the first vowel is usually ———————, and the final *e* is silent.

Guide 2: When a word contains only one vowel, and that vowel is not at the end of the word, the vowel is usually ———————.

Decide how to pronounce each word below. On the line, write the number of the guide that you used to make your decision. Mark each long vowel with a macron (–). Do not mark the short vowels.

	Guide No.		*Guide No.*		*Guide No.*
1. make	——	15. shine	——	29. game	——
2. leg	——	16. clam	——	30. man	——
3. smile	——	17. place	——	31. bite	——
4. grin	——	18. mile	——	32. lock	——
5. hot	——	19. hit	——	33. flame	——
6. mule	——	20. rake	——	34. slip	——
7. land	——	21. mice	——	35. grand	——
8. deck	——	22. pot	——	36. late	——
9. ship	——	23. cube	——	37. stove	——
10. hill	——	24. these	——	38. set	——
11. time	——	25. bride	——	39. rule	——
12. hose	——	26. sun	——	40. crab	——
13. flag	——	27. rope	——		
14. shut	——	28. bed	——		

Lesson 13

Setting

Reading a Literature Selection

▶ Background Information

Have you ever heard of a hang glider? Do you know what it does? A hang glider is a large sail, like a giant kite. The sail has a metal bar connected to it. The wind lifts the sail into the air, and the bar drops down below. A person is held up by a harness or belt attached to the sail. The "pilot" can fly the hang glider by moving the bar. In this story, Angela wants to take a ride on a hang glider.

▶ Skill Focus

Setting is the place and time of the events in a story. Setting tells where and when the events occur. Events can happen in any place and at any time. A story can take place on the streets of a city, in the fields of a farm, or high in the mountains. A story can take place in the present, a hundred years ago, or a hundred years from now. Whatever the setting, it must fit the events in the story.

In some stories, the setting is crucial to the plot. In others, the setting creates an atmosphere, or feeling.

A writer can describe the setting at the beginning of a story or reveal it slowly as the plot develops. As you read, look for words that tell about the setting. Try to picture the place and time of the story.

The following questions will help you understand setting. Ask yourself questions such as the following as you read a story.

1. Where does the story take place?
2. When does it take place?
3. Does the setting fit the events in the story?
4. Why does the setting fit?

▶ Word Clues

The words *like* or *as* can signal a context clue. The words provide a comparison that will help you understand the new word or words. Notice the clue to the meaning of the word *dunes* in the following sentence.

The road ended in sandy white <u>dunes</u> that looked like snowdrifts above the beach.

If you do not know the meaning of the word *dunes*, the phrase *like snowdrifts* can help you. The dunes are compared to snowdrifts using the word *like*. From reading the sentence, you can picture dunes as high piles of white sand that look something like snowdrifts.

Use **comparison** context clues to find the meaning of the three underlined words in the selection.

▶ Strategy Tip

Setting is one of the most important elements of a story. When you read a literature selection, it is important that you understand the story's setting.

As you read "Angela's First Flight," think about whether Angela could hang glide if she lived somewhere else or if she lived many years ago. What are some of the features of the setting that are necessary for hang gliding?

Angela's First Flight

Angela Holland slammed the screen door. "That Paul Daniel!" she shouted. "I can't stand that creep!"

Her mother stood by the kitchen counter. She was slicing bread for lunch. She glanced at Angela.

"Now what happened?" she asked.

Angela flopped down on a kitchen chair.

"He won't let me try his hang glider." Angela rolled her eyes. "You'd think I never had a hang gliding lesson."

"But Angela, you've only had two lessons. You've never flown more than a few feet off the ground."

"But I have my own helmet and gloves. Besides, Paul could teach me. He's been hang gliding for a long time now. And he's had plenty of lessons."

Her mother set the bread and a jar of peanut butter on the table. As Angela sliced a banana for her peanut butter sandwich, her mother listened to her and shook her head.

"Hang gliding is really great, Mom! Once you catch the wind, you glide along on waves of air just like a bird." Angela took a big bite of her sandwich.

When Angela finished her sandwich, she jumped up from the chair, grabbed her helmet and gloves, and headed for the door.

"Thanks for lunch, Mom," she said.

"Where are you going?" her mother asked. "I want you back here by 4:00 to help weed the garden."

"Okay, I'll be back to help." Angela opened the screen door. "I'm going to ride down to the beach."

"Don't do anything foolish, Angela."

As the screen door clapped shut behind her, Angela thought, "There must be some way to get a ride on that glider."

Angela climbed on her bicycle and rode for ten minutes to the beach. All the way she tried to think of ways to get Paul to let her use his glider.

The road ended in sandy white dunes that looked like snowdrifts above the beach. With her equipment in hand, Angela walked to the edge of the dunes. The land dropped off in a steep slope to the beach below. On most days, the wind came in off the ocean. Blowing across the beach, it hit the sandy cliff and rose higher. The rising air was just right for hang gliding.

"Oh no! Are you back?" said Paul. He was standing a little way down the slope.

Angela said nothing as she put on her helmet and gloves. She crossed her legs and sank down on the sand.

The bright blue and green glider lay on the sand next to Paul. He put on his safety helmet. Paul then put on his harness and fastened it to the frame of the glider. Once securely hooked to the glider, Paul lifted it so that the harness straps were tight and tugging at his body. He was now attached to the glider. When the glider took off, he would hang in the air just behind the guide bar.

Paul grabbed the bar and then swung the big wing up over his head and pointed it down the slope. As fast as he could go, Paul ran down the slope, trying all the while to maintain his balance. He was building speed and taking longer and longer strides.

Angela held her breath. The sail filled with air. Within seconds Paul's feet were off the ground. He was lifted higher as the wind caught the hang glider. And then—he sailed along the slope, keeping the glider pointed into the wind and the control bar in the flying position.

Angela cheered and said to herself, "I just have to do it."

Suddenly the nose of the sail pointed up. The back dipped low. The glider had "stalled." Paul and the glider dropped down, bouncing on the sand. He unhooked his harness and took off his helmet. Pulling the glider behind him, Paul <u>trudged</u> up the slope like a tired pack mule.

"What happened?" Angela called out, grinning. "Haven't you learned to fly yet?"

The sun was beating down. Paul was hot, and he was tired from so much gliding. He didn't like people watching him. He had good flights while Angela was away at lunch.

Like an angry lion, Paul <u>glared</u> at Angela. "I bet you couldn't even lift it."

"What!" Angela ground her teeth.

Paul dragged himself up the steep slope. The glider came to a stop. Paul took off his harness and sat down in the sand.

"Bet I can," Angela yelled, jumping up. She grabbed the harness and slipped it on. Then she ran down to the glider and hooked the harness to the frame as her instructor had

shown her. She lifted the glider off the ground. With the control bar in the flying position, Angela began running down the slope.

Paul shouted, but Angela didn't hear what he said. The glider wasn't heavy, but it tipped to one side. She lost her footing and tumbled to the ground. The glider dug into the sand and tipped over.

Angela's mouth was full of sand. Sand was in her eyes and hair, too. She heard Paul laughing from up the slope. He cupped his hands and shouted, "How's it taste?"

Angela jumped up, brushing the sand from her face. She grabbed the glider's bar.

"Hey, you had a chance! Beat it!" shouted Paul. But Angela had the glider over her head and was running down the slope again. The wind rushed past her face. The ocean roared in her ears. She remembered what her instructor had said: "Don't think about flying. Think about running to the bottom of the hill."

Paul's voice came after her. "Tear that sail and you'll pay for it!"

Angela raced down the slope. She was going fast. Each step got longer and longer. Her legs could barely keep up. She started to stumble again. Then she felt a strong tug on the handle. Her feet came off the ground. She was in the air!

The world seemed to fall away. Angela floated slowly along the face of the cliff. The ocean's roar seemed far off. A seagull drifted by right next to her.

Angela leaned toward the ocean side. The wing tipped that way and began a slow, silent turn over the beach.

> *Angela tried to remember how to land. But it was too late.*

Angela could hardly breathe. Her heart pounded with excitement. She loved this feeling of freedom. And flying was so easy.

The glider turned back toward the cliff. Suddenly, Angela was afraid. She had never landed from such a height. Her instructor had warned about wind currents and rotors. Angela felt her fear turning to panic.

The glider was heading straight for the sandy cliff. Angela tried to remember how to land. But it was too late. The wing tip dug into the sand with a <u>jolt</u> as sudden as a flash of lightning. Angela hit the sand hard before coming to a stop.

Angela shook her head and opened her eyes. Her side hurt. Slowly, she looked around. She saw Paul running down the slope toward her and his glider. He glared at Angela and then turned to check the sail.

"You're lucky, Angela," said Paul. "Everything was fine until you landed. You need more lessons. Maybe I can give you some tips."

Paul started to explain to Angela what she did wrong. "You must remember this rule: If you try to keep the hang glider on the ground as you run down the hill, you will have a better takeoff. If you try to keep the hang glider in the air as you land, you will have a good landing."

Angela listened to Paul attentively. He was absolutely right about takeoffs and landings. She knew that once she finished her lessons, Paul would give her another try. She realized now how foolish she had been to take Paul's glider. She was lucky that she hadn't been seriously hurt. Next time, though, her landing would be perfect.

1. What is a hang glider?

   _____

   _____

2. How does it fly?

   _____

   _____

   _____

3. How many hang gliding lessons has Angela had?

   _____

4. What equipment must a hang glider pilot have?

   _____

   _____

5. Why is the beach a good place for hang gliding?

   _____

   _____

   _____

6. What drifts right by Angela on her flight?

   _____

7. Was Angela's second attempt to hang glide more or less successful than her first? Explain.

   _____

   _____

   _____

   _____

   _____

8. What must Angela do before Paul will let her have another ride on his glider?

   _____

9. Complete each sentence with the correct word from below.

   glared   jolt   trudged

   a. Robert had trouble pulling the sled as he _____ through the snow.

   b. The _____ of the car hitting a tree threw the driver forward in his seat.

   c. Lisa _____ at her brother when he used her computer without permission.

1. How does Mrs. Holland feel about Angela's wanting to hang glide?

   _____

   _____

2. Do you think Paul is a selfish person? Explain.

   _____

   _____

3. How does Angela feel about her first flight with a hang glider?

   _____

4. How could hang gliding be dangerous?

_____

_____

5. Do you think that Angela would try new sports as she discovered them? Explain.

_____

_____

6. a. Describe what you would see if you were flying the hang glider over the beach.

_____

_____

   b. Would a person on the ground watching you see the same things? Explain.

_____

_____

7. Could Angela have gone hang gliding if she lived in an inland city? Explain.

_____

_____

SKILL FOCUS

Below are the questions you were asked to think about as you read the story.
Write your answers on the lines provided.

1. Where does the story take place?

_____

2. When does it take place?

_____

3. Does the setting fit the events in the story?

_____

4. Why does the setting fit?

_____

_____

5. Could you hang glide where you live? Why? Why not?

_____

_____

▶ **Real Life Connections** Would you like to try hang gliding? Why or why not?

Reading a Map

Reading a Social Studies Selection

▶ Background Information

For years, Russia and the United States have competed with one another to be the first country in space and the first country to land on the moon. The competition began when Russia launched its first unmanned satellite, *Sputnik I*, meaning *traveler*, into space on October 4, 1957.

In 1961, a Russian cosmonaut and an American astronaut were the first people to travel in space. Yuri Gagarin was the first to go into orbit around Earth. Alan Shepard's flight was about a month later. Since that time, there have been many historic space flights. In 1969, American astronaut Neil A. Armstrong climbed out of Apollo II to the moon's surface. He was the first human to set foot on the moon. In 1975, the United States and Russia cooperated on their first joint mission—an Apollo spacecraft docked with a Soyuz craft in space. During the *Atlantis-Mir* mission in 1995, Americans and Russians soared together in space again.

▶ Skill Focus

When reading about different parts of the world, you may want to use a globe to see where these places are located. A globe, however, may not be nearby. That is why some of your textbooks include **maps.** A map can show you the whole world at one time or only a part of the world.

There are many important things to look for on a map. You should first look at the **title** of the map or the caption under the map. The caption or title tells what the map shows. Another important feature is the **compass,** which shows the directions north, south, east, and west. A compass tells you the direction from one place on the map to another.

On a map of the world, also be sure to look for the **equator.** The equator is an imaginary circle around the earth that divides the world into the Northern Hemisphere and the Southern Hemisphere.

You can often find other information on maps, such as the names of cities, countries, bodies of water, and so on. Together, the map and the selection give you more information than either one could provide alone.

▶ Word Clues

Read the sentences below. Look for the context clues that explain the underlined word.

> Then they joined in a celebration and exchanged <u>offerings.</u> These gifts included flowers, fruit, and chocolates from *Atlantis*. *Mir* offered the traditional Russian gifts of bread and salt.

If you do not know the meaning of the word *offerings* in the first sentence, read the next sentence. The words *these gifts* explain the meaning of *offerings*.

Use **definition** context clues to find the meaning of the three underlined words in the selection.

▶ Strategy Tip

When you read a social studies selection, such as "The *Atlantis-Mir* Mission," it is important to look at the maps. Look at the map on page 43. Read the title and the compass. Also locate the equator.

The *Atlantis-Mir* Mission

Robert Gibson had his hand on a joystick, a control stick in the craft. His eyes were on a television screen. Everything had to go just right. Even a few inches made a difference.

Gibson was 245 miles above Earth. He was commander of the American space shuttle *Atlantis*. And his spacecraft was moving toward the Russian space station *Mir*. If all went well, the two orbiting spacecrafts would soon dock in space. When spacecrafts dock, they join in space. But if *Atlantis* bumped *Mir* too hard, both of the spaceships and the people aboard could be in danger.

Gibson gently moved *Atlantis* into position. *Atlantis* had a camera in the middle of its docking fixture. This technology allowed Gibson to watch what was happening on a TV screen. *Atlantis* floated toward *Mir*, foot by foot, inch by inch. Latches and hooks locked into place. And an American spaceship and a Russian one flew in space together.

Gibson had brought the two crafts together within two seconds of the planned time. Linked together, they became the largest structure people had ever placed in orbit. Millions watched the docking on live television. Both spacecrafts were beaming pictures back to Earth. Pictures from *Mir* showed *Atlantis* astronauts waving through overhead windows as the spaceships moved closer together.

Atlantis had left Cape Canaveral, Florida, on June 27, 1995. About two days later, the successful docking took place. The spaceships docked over central Russia, near the Russian and Mongolian border.

Mir had been in orbit since 1986, but the crew of the space station had been rotated. When crews are rotated, a spaceship brings a new crew to the craft and returns the old crew to Earth.

Russian–American Teams

Americans and Russians had begun working together even before the docking took place. *Atlantis* and *Mir* each carried American astronauts and Russian cosmonauts.

The American aboard *Mir* was Dr. Norman Thagard. After training in Russia, he had spent three months on *Mir* before the docking with *Atlantis*. The Russians aboard *Mir* were Commander Vladimir Dezhurov and Gennady Strekalov.

In addition to Commander Gibson, *Atlantis* carried four other Americans, two women and two men. They were Ellen Baker, Bonnie Dunbar, Charles Precourt, and Greg Harbaugh. The Russians on *Atlantis* were Anatoly Solovyev and Nikolai Budarin.

Anniversary in Space

After docking, crew members spent the first two hours checking for leaks. Then Gibson opened a hatch to meet Commander Dezhurov. The Russian grabbed Gibson's hand as he greeted him joyfully.

The crews could now go back and forth in a passageway between the two crafts. Because there is no gravity in space, people are weightless. The crews could simply float as they moved about the spacecrafts. The men gathered in the *Mir* to take pictures. Then they celebrated their joint mission and exchanged offerings. These gifts included flowers, fruit, and chocolates from *Atlantis*. *Mir* offered the traditional Russian gifts of bread and salt.

This celebration was not just for the successful docking. It was also an anniversary. Twenty years before, in 1975, Americans and Russians docked in space for the first time. On that mission, the U.S. Apollo docked with the USSR Soyuz. The two crews worked together for two days.

Now, at the second docking in space, Gibson spoke in Russian. "Today we're reaffirming our friendship after the flight of *Apollo-Soyuz*," he said. "Together we will build a future based on cooperation, mutual trust and friendship."

> Atlantis *and* Mir *each carried American astronauts and Russian cosmonauts.*

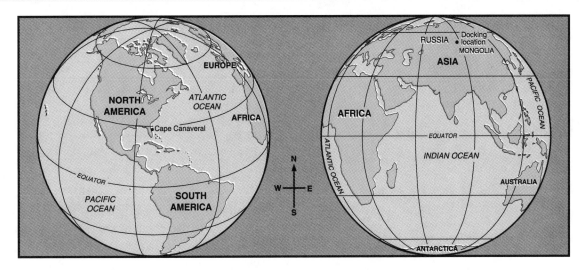

Working Together in Space

After the celebrations, the crews got to work. First, they carried food and water from the *Atlantis* to the *Mir* to replace the *Mir*'s supplies. Then they began the experiments that they would do during their five days together.

The shuttle's Spacelab module held a laboratory about the size of a bus. This lab was used for many tests to study how space flight affects the body. All ten people were tested, especially those on the *Mir*. Because they had been in orbit several months, both crews were tested for the long-term effects of space flight.

The crews also hoped they would learn information that would help people on Earth. For example, many people suffer from a bone condition called osteoporosis (OSS tee o pə RO səs). People with this condition lose bone mass. The bones then break very easily. While astronauts are in space, where there is no gravity, they lose bone mass. Because calcium builds bones, tests were done on how the body uses calcium while weightless. Scientists would be able to use the information from the tests as they studied bone conditions on Earth.

The *Atlantis-Mir* mission was an important first step in a long-term plan. The United States and Russia will continue to work together on missions in space. *Mir* remained in orbit, and several more *Atlantis-Mir* dockings are planned. There are also plans for a new space station, with other countries joining the effort.

Undocking

After five days in space, the two spaceships were ready to undock. Before separating, they exchanged some crew members. The crew on *Mir*, including Dr. Thagard, came aboard the *Atlantis*. The two Russians on *Atlantis* boarded the *Mir*. They would continue in orbit until they were replaced by another crew.

The astronauts and cosmonauts were almost tearful as they said good-bye. Charles Precourt said, "I feel very small . . . when I look back at Earth through the window, I see a giant planet. Together we can do anything. . . . We can even fly to Mars."

Return to Earth

After the undocking, *Atlantis* returned to Cape Canaveral. The eight people landed safely on July 7, 1995. Dr. Thagard had been in space for nearly four months. He had set a new record for the longest space flight for an American. President Clinton called from the White House to congratulate him.

NASA doctors expected Dr. Thagard to be wobbly after his long flight. But they were surprised when he walked from the space shuttle. The doctors tested Dr. Thagard and his two crewmates from *Mir* for nearly a month. The tests, along with those done in space, will help them study the effects of long space flights.

President Clinton also spoke with Commander Gibson. "This is truly the beginning of a new era of cooperation in space between the United States and Russia," President Clinton said. "We're doing things together, and I think what you and your team and . . . the Russians did together symbolize that more than anything that I could ever say."

Along with congratulations, one astronaut received a special treat. Dr. Thagard had been promised ice cream. And that is what he got after his long journey into space.

1. Tell the names of the American space shuttle and the Russian space station.

_____

_____

2. How many miles above Earth were the spaceships?

_____

3. How could Commander Gibson watch what was happening as he prepared for docking?

_____

_____

_____

4. Was this the first time Americans and Russians had docked in space? Explain.

_____

5. What caused the crews to float in space?

_____

_____

6. What was Spacelab used for?

_____

_____

7. Why were the people on the *Mir* tested?

_____

_____

8. Tests were done on how the body uses calcium while weightless. How could scientists use these tests to help people on Earth?

_____

_____

9. Tell, in order, the main events that occurred after the crews had spent five days in space.

_____

_____

_____

10. Write the letter of the correct meaning in front of each word.

_____ joy stick   **a.** join

_____ dock   **b.** brought something new to replace something else

_____ rotated   **c.** control stick

INTERPRETING FACTS

1. Think about the astronauts and cosmonauts who worked together in space. What qualities did they need to have?

_____

_____

2. How do you think the astronauts and cosmonauts felt as they prepared to undock?

_____

_____

3. When Dr. Thagard walked from the shuttle at Cape Canaveral, he was not wobbly as doctors had expected. What conclusions can you draw about the effect of several months in space on the astronaut?

_____

_____

S KILL   FOCUS

Use the maps of the world on page 43 to answer these questions. If necessary, look back at the selection.

1. Find the point on the map from which *Atlantis* started. What is the name of this place?

_____

2. On what continent is this place located?

_____

3. What ocean is nearby?

_____

4. *Atlantis* and *Mir* docked in space above a place shown on the map. What is the name of this place?

_____

5. On what continent is this place located?

_____

6. What ocean is to the east of this continent?

_____

7. What continent is to the southwest?

_____

8. What continent is to the southeast?

_____

9. Did the spaceships dock north or south of the equator?

_____

10. Use the maps to plan a docking in space. Choose a place over which the spaceships will dock. Tell the name of the continent and its location in relation to oceans, other continents, and the equator.

_____

_____

▶ **Real Life Connections** Name another endeavor in which you feel the Americans and the Russians could work together today. Give reasons for your response.

Diagrams

— Reading a Science Selection

▶ Background Information

Whoosh! The hot-air balloon rises. You float silently above the earth. How does the balloon work? How can hot air keep hundreds of pounds up in the sky? This selection uses both words and diagrams to show how balloons work.

As you read "Balloons and Airships," look carefully at the diagrams. Remember to go back and forth between the paragraphs and the diagrams.

▶ Skill Focus

Drawings, or **diagrams**, are often used in textbooks to show what the words in a selection explain. Diagrams are usually called Figure 1, Figure 2, and so on. When reading a selection with diagrams, read the text first. Then look at the diagram that shows what the words explain.

When you read diagrams, be sure to read the **labels**. Labels name the parts of the diagram. Often a **caption** will appear with a diagram. Read it before you study the diagram. It will often be helpful to read the explanation in the selection again. Going back and forth from the words in the selection to the diagram will help you to understand the ideas.

When you read a selection that has diagrams, use the following steps.

1. Read the paragraph before each diagram. Then study the diagram and read the caption that goes with it. If there are labels, read them while studying the diagram. The paragraph below the diagram may explain what is pictured. Read that paragraph, too.
2. Slowly read the rest of the paragraphs. Look back at the diagrams when you think they will help you.
3. After you have finished reading and studying the diagrams, look away from the selection. Try to picture what you have read and the details in the diagrams. If you cannot do this, read the paragraphs and study the diagrams again.
4. Continue to work in this way until you understand all the ideas in the selection.

▶ Word Clues

Read the sentence below. Look for context clues that explain the underlined word.

Every material has a certain <u>density</u>, or thickness of matter.

If you do not know the meaning of the word *density*, the phrase *thickness of matter* can help you. Density is thickness of matter. The phrase *thickness of matter* is an appositive phrase. An appositive phrase explains a word coming before it and is set off from the word by commas or dashes and the word *or*.

Use **appositive phrases** to find the meaning of the three underlined words in the selection.

▶ Strategy Tip

When reading a science selection it is particulary helpful to look carefully at the diagrams. As you read "Balloons and Airships," remember to go back and forth between the paragraphs and the diagrams.

BALLOONS AND AIRSHIPS

How Do Things Float?

A balloon is known as a "lighter-than-air craft." How can this be? We know that air is lighter than almost anything. A balloon—cloth, rope, wood, steel, and other things—must be heavier! A balloon can't really be "lighter" than air. So, what keeps it up?

Every material has a certain density, or thickness of matter. This term means that the basic building blocks—the molecules—can be closer together or farther apart. Air is not very dense. Rocks and steel are quite dense.

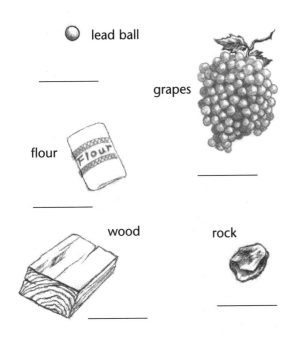

Figure 1. This diagram shows various materials and how much space a kilogram of each material will take up.

Imagine a pound of air and a pound of rocks. Which one would be bigger? In Figure 1, you can see pictures of several items. They all weigh the same. Which is the biggest? Which is the smallest? Which is the most dense? Which is the least dense?

If you heat up air, it becomes less dense. The molecules move around a lot more when the air is hot. The moving molecules take up more space. If you fill a balloon with hot air, the air in the balloon is less dense than the air outside the balloon. What happens? Figure 2 shows that denser air around the balloon

Figure 2. The air around the balloon is denser. It tries to move into the space that the balloon takes up. The balloon is forced upward because it is lighter than the amount of air that would fill the same space.

pushes in against it and forces it upward. If the upward force is more than the weight of the balloon and the air inside it, the balloon will float upward.

How Does a Hot-Air Balloon Work?

A hot-air balloon has several parts, as you can see in Figure 3. The **bag** is made of strong cloth like nylon. The cloth is covered with rubber to keep it from leaking. A net of ropes on the outside of the bag helps to keep its shape

Figure 3. Parts of a hot-air balloon.

and supports the **basket** or **gondola** below. The bottom of the balloon is called the **neck**. Hanging inside the neck is a propane burner for heating the air.

A balloonist makes the balloon rise by heating the air at the neck. The hot air is less dense and rises into the bag. As hot air enters the bag, the colder air inside is forced out of the neck. When the bag has expanded enough, it begins to float. Soon the balloon, with its burner, basket, and passengers, rises into the air. The balloonist can then shut off the burner.

✔ As the air in the balloon begins to cool, the air in it takes up less space. The air around the balloon has less to push on, so the balloon begins to come down. The balloonist can control the rising and sinking of the balloon very precisely by running the burner and shutting it off. Short bursts of hot air can keep the balloon at one level. Longer bursts can make it rise.

How Does a Gas Balloon Work?

Some gases are much less dense than air. Helium—or a relatively expensive gas—is much less dense than air. It is suitable for use in balloons. In Figure 4, you can see a helium balloon. It looks a lot like the hot-air balloon. What parts are the same? What parts are different? The balloonist cannot control the temperature of the gas. How does the balloon go up and down?

Once the helium gas is pumped into the bag, the balloon begins to rise. Ballast, or weights that control the height of the balloon,

hang around the outside of the basket to weigh it down. The balloonist dumps some of the sand to make the balloon rise. When the balloon is at the right height, the balloonist can open a **valve** at the top of the bag to spill out some of the gas. The open valve makes the balloon stop rising.

The balance between the gas and the weight of the balloon is very fine. If the balloonist dumps out a few handfuls of sand, the balloon will rise very quickly. If the balloonist opens the valve for just a few seconds, the balloon will sink very quickly.

How Do You Steer a Balloon?

If you let a toy helium balloon go, it will rise and be carried away by the wind. The same thing happens with hot-air and gas balloons. Balloonists must plan carefully. They get weather reports and make sure that the wind will carry them where they want to go. You can imagine that balloons are not very efficient for transportation.

There are other kinds of balloons, called **airships**. Airships have motors and propellers on them so that they can go in any direction. A dirigible, or an airship that can be steered, was once a means of transportation. Some dirigibles even crossed the ocean. Now they are used mostly to carry advertising or to provide a bird's-eye view at sporting events.

Figure 5 shows several types of balloons and airships. Which ones are dirigibles? Which ones can carry passengers?

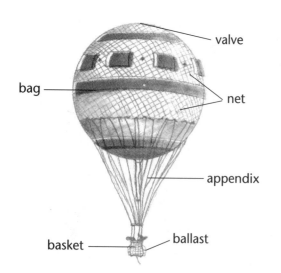

Figure 4. Parts of a gas balloon.

Figure 5. Different kinds of balloons and airships.

RECALLING FACTS

1. Which is denser, feathers or wood?

   _____

2. What happens when you heat air?

   _____

3. Find the paragraph that has a check mark next to it. Underline the sentence that tells the main idea.

4. Write the meaning of each word.

   helium _____

   _____

   dirigible _____

   _____

   ballast _____

   _____

INTERPRETING FACTS

1. What advantage does a dirigible have over a hot-air balloon?

   _____

2. What would limit the amount of time you could spend on a hot-air balloon ride?

   _____

   _____

   _____

3. What would limit the amount of time you could spend on a helium balloon ride?

   _____

   _____

SKILL FOCUS

1. In Figure 1, number the materials according to how dense they are. Use *1* for the densest material.

2. List any items in Figure 3 that are missing from Figure 4. _____

3. List any items in Figure 4 that are missing from Figure 3. _____

4. In Figure 5, put an X by the balloons that can be steered. Put a check mark by the balloons that can carry people.

▶ **Real Life Connections** In your opinion, are hot-air balloons safe? Tell why or why not.

Metric Terms and Symbols

Reading a Mathematics Selection

▶ Background Information

Did you know that in 1670, Frenchman Gabriel Mouton proposed a decimal system? One year later, Jean Picard, a French astronomer proposed that the unit of measure be based on the swing of a pendulum. Over the next 120 years, many others proposed various systems.

In 1790, Thomas Jefferson suggested that the United States use a decimal measurement system. Congress rejected this recommendation. At the same time in France, the metric system was being created.

In 1821, Secretary of State John Quincy Adams also thought that the United States should convert to a decimal system. However, at the time, the United States traded mostly with Canada and Great Britain. The United States, Canada, and Great Britain all used the English System. At the time, these three countries believed that there was no need to change their system.

You are already familiar with the English system. It uses many of the units from the U.S.

Customary System. The problem with the English system is that it is haphazard; it doesn't follow a specific pattern. For instance, twelve inches equals one foot, while three feet equals one yard. Unless a person is familiar with the system, it is very difficult to follow.

Since 1790, the world has gradually converted to the metric system. Canada and Great Britain were among the last countries to change over to this system. Once this took place, the United States evaluated the situation and decided on a gradual shift to the metric system. This is why it is important for you to learn the metric system.

▶ Skill Focus

A group of French scientists created the metric system in the 1790s. Why did they decide to use the metric system? Until that time, each country had its own language of measurement. This made it difficult for scientists from different countries to communicate. Finally, some scientists decided to make one system of measurement. This made it easier to compare the work of scientists from different countries.

The metric system is simple to use. To change from one unit of length to the next smaller unit in the metric system, divide by 10. To go from one unit to the next larger unit, multiply by 10.

▶ Word Clues

When working with metric measurements, you will come across the following three words: *meter, gram,* and *liter.* Prefixes can be added to these words to change their meanings. Some of these prefixes are *kilo, hecto, deca, deci, centi,* and *milli.*

▶ Strategy Tip

The **metric system** is a system of measurement that is used around the world. You know many of the labels that are used in the English system, such as inches, feet, pounds, and miles. The metric system also has special labels that you need to know. In "Metric Base Units and Prefixes," you will learn some of those words and some special prefixes.

Metric Base Units and Prefixes

Base Units

There are seven base units in the metric system. Most everyday measurements can be done with only three of these units.

To measure length, use the **meter.** A meter is about the length of a baseball bat.

To measure weight, use the **gram.** A gram is about the weight of a dollar bill.

To measure volume, use the **liter.** A liter of milk is about as much as a quart of milk.

Metric Prefixes

Larger and smaller units in the metric system are named by adding prefixes to the base units. You know that a prefix can change the meaning of a root word. In the metric system, several prefixes are used with each of the three base units. Prefixes are added to the units meter, gram, and liter to change their meanings. Following are six prefixes for you to learn. Knowing these prefixes can help you unlock the meaning of most words in the metric system.

kilo	1,000 times larger
hecto	100 times larger
deca	10 times larger
deci	10 times smaller
centi	100 times smaller
milli	1,000 times smaller

A **hectometer** (HEK tə meet ər) is 100 times longer than a meter. That means that a hectometer is about the length of 100 baseball bats put end to end. A hectometer is a little longer than a football field.

A **milliliter** (MIL ə leet ər) is 1,000 times smaller than a liter. A milliliter of water is only a few drops.

A **kilogram** (KIL ə gram) is 1,000 times heavier than a gram. A brick weighs about one kilogram.

Symbols

There are symbols that stand for the metric units and the prefixes. This means that the whole word does not have to be written each time. Notice that the symbols do not have periods after them. Notice also that only the symbol for liter is capitalized.

Prefixes				*Units*	
kilo	**k**	deci	**d**	meter	**m**
hecto	**h**	centi	**c**	liter	**l**
deca	**da**	milli	**m**	gram	**g**

The symbols for the prefixes and units can be combined. The symbol for kilogram is *kg,* the symbol for **decaliter** (DEK ə leet ər) is *daL,* and so on.

As you learn to use the metric system, these units will be easier for you to recognize. For now, the most important thing is to remember what each unit measures and to get a feeling for the size of the measures.

1. How many base units are in the metric system?

   _____

2. How many base units are commonly used for measurements?

   _____

   _____

3. What are the names of the three base units in the metric system?

   _____ _____ _____

4. Many metric words are formed by adding

   a _____ to a base unit.

Put a check mark next to the words that complete each of the following sentences.

5. When the prefixes *kilo*, *hecto*, and *deca* are added to a base unit, the measurement is

   _____ the same as the base unit.

   _____ larger than the base unit.

   _____ smaller than the base unit.

6. When the prefixes *deci*, *centi*, and *milli* are added to a base unit, the measurement is

   _____ the same as the base unit.

   _____ larger than the base unit.

   _____ smaller than the base unit.

INTERPRETING FACTS

1. All the prefixes that make the base unit smaller end in what letter? _____

2. All the prefixes that make the base unit larger end in what letters? _____

3. How does knowing the meaning of the prefix *kilo* help you understand the word *kilometer*?

   _____

4. What might happen if a country chose not to use the metric system?

   _____

SKILL FOCUS

A. Write *meters*, *liters*, or *grams* on the lines provided.

1. In 1903, an airplane flew for 12 seconds. It flew about 37 _____.

2. The Lockheed C-5A Galaxy can carry 110,000 kilo _____ of cargo.

3. The Hindenberg was about the length of 30 buses, about 245 _____.

4. The steward served 200 milli _____ of coffee to each passenger.

5. In 1908, an airplane flew for 1 minute and 28 seconds. It flew about 1 kilo _____.

6. The fuel gauge showed the pilot that she had 47 _____ of fuel left.

B. Write the symbol for the following measures on the lines provided. Remember that only the symbol *L* is capitalized. You may look back at the selection to find an answer.

1. kilometer _____   4. decagram _____   7. milliliter _____

2. milligram _____   5. centimeter _____   8. kilogram _____

3. deciliter _____   6. hectoliter _____   9. decameter _____

Write the word for each symbol on the lines provided.

10. mm _____   13. daL _____   16. cL _____

11. cg _____   14. hm _____   17. hg _____

12. kL _____   15. dg _____   18. dm _____

C. Circle the unit that you would use to measure each of the things pictured.

1. liter / meter

2. gram / meter

3. liter / gram

4. km / L

5. kg / mg

6. m / km

▶ **Real Life Connections** How many meters is it from your room to the refrigerator?

Main Idea

The main idea of a paragraph is not always found in the first sentence.
It is sometimes found in the last sentence.

Read the following paragraphs. Below each one are three sentences from the paragraph. Circle the letter of the sentence that is the main idea of the paragraph.

The Sea Horse

1. The sea horse isn't like most fish. Its head looks like that of a pony. The sea horse has hard, spiny skin. Its tail looks like that of a monkey. It has one fin that isn't much help in swimming. Sea horses drift upright in the water.

   a. The sea horse has hard, spiny skin.
   b. Its tail looks like that of a monkey.
   c. The sea horse isn't like most fish.

2. The father sea horse has a pocket somewhat like a kangaroo's pouch. He carries the mother's eggs around in this pouch. He even carries the baby sea horses around for some time after they have hatched. The father sea horse takes very good care of his young.

   a. The father sea horse has a pocket somewhat like a kangaroo's pouch.
   b. He carries the mother's eggs around in this pouch.
   c. The father sea horse takes very good care of his young.

The Octopus

3. The octopus has a soft, pouchlike body. It has a head with eyes that look like human eyes. Instead of having fins like a fish, it has eight long arms coming out from its body. Some octopuses have arms nine or ten feet long. Each arm is lined with cuplike suckers. Like the sea horse, the octopus's shape is different from that of most fish.

   a. It has a head with eyes that look like human eyes.
   b. Like the sea horse, the octopus's shape is different from that of most fish.
   c. Some octopuses have arms nine or ten feet long.

4. The octopus uses its arms to get food. It moves along the ocean floor looking for something to eat. When it finds a crab, lobster, or fish, the octopus wraps its arms around the victim. The suckers on the octopus's arms hold the animal as the arms draw the food to the mouth.

   a. When it finds a crab, lobster, or fish, the octopus wraps its arms around the victim.
   b. The octopus uses its arms to get food.
   c. It moves along the ocean floor looking for something to eat.

The Giant Clam

5. The giant clam is an interesting sea creature. The giant clam is the largest of all clams. It sometimes weighs as much as 500 pounds. Its shell may measure four feet across. This clam is not found in American waters. It lives in the warm waters of the Indian and Pacific oceans.

   a. This clam is not found in American waters.
   b. The giant clam is an interesting sea creature.
   c. It sometimes weighs as much as 500 pounds.

6. The giant clam's shell consists of two parts. Each part is used as a huge storage area for water and food. The clam can snap the two parts of its shell together with great force. It is said that divers have been caught and injured in this great shell. The clam's shell is both useful and dangerous.

   a. The clam's shell is both useful and dangerous.
   b. The giant clam's shell consists of two parts.
   c. It is said that divers have been caught and injured in this great shell.

Main Idea

In many paragraphs you read, the main idea is in the first or last sentence of the paragraph. However, the main idea doesn't always appear in these sentences. It can sometimes be found in any of the sentences in between.

Read the following paragraphs. Below each one are three sentences from the paragraph. Circle the letter of the sentence that is the main idea of the paragraph.

1. Birds are alike in many ways. All of them are vertebrates because they have backbones. All birds have two legs and two wings. All birds have feathers and lungs. Birds are warmblooded. *Warmblooded* means "their bodies are warm even when the weather is cold."

    a. All birds have feathers and lungs.
    b. Birds are alike in many ways.
    c. Birds are warmblooded.

2. Some birds, like the ostrich, are taller and heavier than a person. Some are very small, like the hummingbird. Some hummingbirds are the length of a person's finger. Many birds, such as swallows and ducks, are good flyers. Some birds cannot fly at all. The penguin's wings cannot lift the penguin off the ground. There are many different kinds of birds.

    a. Some birds, like the ostrich, are taller and heavier than a person.
    b. The penguin's wings cannot lift the penguin off the ground.
    c. There are many different kinds of birds.

3. The outer feathers of birds form a smooth covering for their bodies. The down feathers next to their bodies help to keep in body heat. Their wing feathers are used for flying. Their tail feathers help them in balancing or in steering. Not only does each feather type have a purpose, but the feathers can be replaced. Birds usually shed their old, worn-out feathers in the fall and grow a new set. Shedding of feathers is known as molting.

    a. Not only does each feather type have a purpose, but the feathers can be replaced.
    b. Shedding of feathers is known as molting.
    c. Their wing feathers are used for flying.

4. Birds weigh very little because their bones are thin-walled and hollow. Their feathers are also very light. Flying birds have powerful muscles attached to the breastbone. The bodies of most birds are built for flying.

    a. Birds weigh very little because their bones are thin-walled and hollow.
    b. Their feathers are also very light.
    c. The bodies of most birds are built for flying.

5. Birds' eggs must be kept warm. The baby bird grows inside the egg, eating up the food stored in the egg. By the time the food is used up, the bird fills the whole egg. Then it comes out of the egg, or hatches. All birds develop in eggs. Large birds, such as ostriches, lay eggs that are often as large as six inches long. Tiny birds, such as hummingbirds, lay eggs that are each only a quarter of an inch long.

    a. All birds develop in eggs.
    b. Birds' eggs must be kept warm.
    c. Tiny birds, such as hummingbirds, lay eggs that are each only a quarter of an inch long.

6. Certain birds serve as symbols. For example, many people regard the owl as a symbol of wisdom. The dove is often a symbol of peace. The eagle can be a symbol of political and military power. The bald eagle, which lives only in North America, is the national symbol of the United States.

    a. The dove is often a symbol of peace.
    b. Certain birds serve as symbols.
    c. The bald eagle, which lives only in North America, is the national symbol of the United States.

Lesson 19

Consonant Blends

Some **consonant blends** have three letters. Three consonants are blended together in such a way that the consonant sound each stands for is heard.

scr   shr   spl   spr   squ   str   thr

Say each picture name. Listen to the beginning sounds. On the line, write the blend listed above that stands for the consonant sounds that you hear at the beginning of the picture name.

1. strawberry _____

2. squirrel _____

3. screw _____

4. shrub _____

5. spring _____

6. three _____

7. splinter _____

8. square _____

9. shrimp _____

10. splash _____

11. spruce _____

12. string _____

13. squirt _____

14. throne _____

15. scrub _____

16. sprinkle _____

17. shrug _____

18. thread _____

19. stream _____

20. split _____

21. scream _____

22. squash _____

23. spray _____

24. strap _____

25. throw _____

26. screen _____

27. shrunk _____

28. splint _____

29. strainer _____

30. scroll _____

31. squeeze _____

32. throat _____

Consonant Digraphs

Say the word *shadow* and listen to its beginning sound. You hear only one sound at the beginning of the word. When two letters stand for one sound, as in *sh*, the two letters are called a **consonant digraph**.

ch   ph   sh   th   wh

Say each picture name. Listen to the beginning sound. On the line, write the digraph listed above that stands for the sound that you hear at the beginning of the picture name.

1. sheep
2. chair
3. wheel
4. thermometer
5. phone
6. whistle
7. thimble
8. shell
9. cheese
10. photograph
11. whale
12. shoe
13. chicken
14. phonograph
15. thumb
16. shark

Say each picture name. Listen to the ending sound. On the line, write the digraph listed above that stands for the sound that you hear at the end of the picture name.

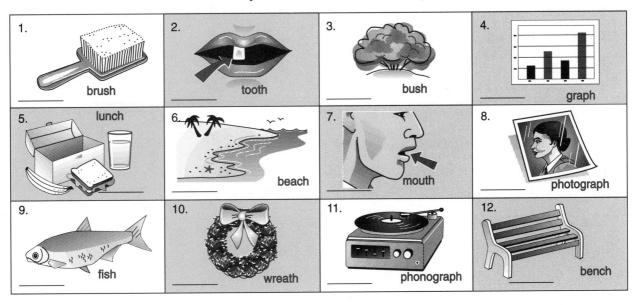

1. brush
2. tooth
3. bush
4. graph
5. lunch
6. beach
7. mouth
8. photograph
9. fish
10. wreath
11. phonograph
12. bench

*Lesson 21*_____

Long Vowel Sounds

You have had practice in working with one-syllable words with and without a final *e.* You have learned two guides to use in deciding whether the first vowel sound in such words is long or short.

There is another guide that you can use to decide if a vowel is long. See if you can discover this guide for yourself.

Words with Two Vowels Together

Write a one-word answer to each question. The first one has been done for you.

	How many vowels are there together?	Which vowel has a long sound?	Which vowel is silent?
1. boat	two	first	second
2. real			
3. wait			
4. heal			
5. roast			
6. soap			

Fill in the words necessary to complete the following guide.

> **Guide 3:** When two _____ come together in a word, the first _____ is usually _____, and the second is usually _____.

Read each sentence below. Look for a word in each sentence that has two vowels together. Say this word softly. Circle the vowel that has a long sound.

1. Tom went to Maine to spend the summer months.
2. He liked the sea.
3. He can swim and he can float.
4. His father has a boat.
5. They often went for a sail.
6. One day Tom invited some children to a party at the beach.
7. It started to rain but stopped by lunchtime.
8. They had a corn roast.
9. Afterward, they had fresh peaches.
10. Finally, they had vanilla ice cream.

Long and Short Vowel Sounds

The three guides that you have learned to help you decide whether the vowel sound in a one-syllable word is short or long are given below with a word or words missing in each one. Write a word on each line to complete the three guides.

Guide 1: When a word contains two vowels, one of which is a final *e*, the first vowel is usually _____, and the final *e* is silent.

Guide 2: When a word contains only one vowel, and that vowel is not at the end of the word, the vowel is usually _____.

Guide 3: When two vowels come together in a word, the first vowel is usually _____, and the second vowel is usually _____.

Decide how to pronounce each word below. On the line, write the number of the guide that you used in making your decision. Mark each long vowel with a macron (–). Do not mark the short vowels.

Guide No.	*Guide No.*	*Guide No.*
1. wage _____	13. grain _____	25. ride _____
2. drove _____	14. road _____	26. home _____
3. truck _____	15. rush _____	27. load _____
4. bean _____	16. take _____	28. while _____
5. grape _____	17. eat _____	29. gain _____
6. pea _____	18. rain _____	30. trim _____
7. man _____	19. tank _____	31. feast _____
8. these _____	20. time _____	32. same _____
9. each _____	21. shed _____	33. reap _____
10. ice _____	22. job _____	34. still _____
11. fresh _____	23. meal _____	35. lake _____
12. team _____	24. late _____	36. float _____

Using a Train Schedule

Many people travel to work every day on trains. Most commuter trains follow a **schedule**, a printed timetable of arrivals and/or departures. People who commute every day at the same time do not need to think much about train schedules. However, shoppers, visitors, and workers without fixed work times often look at a train schedule so that they can plan their travel.

Study the portion of a train schedule below. It gives information about trains that travel from Franklin to Boston, Massachusetts. The headings at the top of each column tell what kind of information is given in each column. Notice the abbreviations and special symbols. Explanations are listed at the bottom of the schedule.

INBOUND	Train No.	700	702	704	706	708*	752
READ DOWN		A.M.	A.M.	A.M.	A.M.	A.M.	A.M.
Dep: Forge Park	O	5:15	5:45	6:15	6:33	7:06	
Franklin	O	5:22	5:52	6:22	6:42	7:13	
Norfolk		5:29	5:59	6:29	6:49	7:20	
Walpole	O	5:35	6:05	6:35	6:55	7:27	
Windsor Gardens		5:39	6:09	6:39	7:01	7:31	
Norwood Central	O	5:43	6:13	6:43	7:05	7:36	7:58
Norwood Depot		5:46	6:16		7:08		8:01
Islington		5:49	6:19		7:11		8:04
Dedham Corporate Ctr.		5:52	6:22	6:48	7:14	7:42	8:07
Endicott		5:55	6:26		7:18		8:11
Readville		6:00	6:29		7:21		8:15
Ruggles	T			7:00	7:32	7:56	
Back Bay	T, O		L6:43	L7:04	L7:36	L8:00	
Arr: South Station, Boston	T, O	6:20	6:48	7:09	7:41	8:05	8:35

SYMBOLS

L: Regular stop to discharge or pick up passengers but train may leave ahead of schedule.
O: Ticket outlet is located at or near station.
T: Subway connection.

Handicapped accessibility at Forge Park, Norfolk, Norwood Central, Norwood Depot, Dedham Corporate Ctr., Ruggles, Back Bay, and South Station.
Train 706 stops at Plimptonville at 6:38 A.M.
Shaded portion denotes peak service.
* Train does not operate on Martin Luther King Day, Columbus Day, and Veterans Day.

A. Write the answer to each question on the line.

1. What is the number of the earliest train you can take from Forge Park? _____

2. At which stations can you connect with the subway system? _____

_____

3. At what station does Train 752 begin? _____

4. What is the number of the train that is not in the peak service area? _____

5. What time does Train 704 leave Walpole? _____

6. What is the number of the train that leaves Endicott at 7:18 A.M.? _____

7. Which train can't you take on Veterans Day? _____

8. At which station could a train leave early? _____

9. Where can you connect with the subway but not buy tickets? _____

10. Which train makes the fewest stops? _____

11. What time do you have to leave Franklin to get to South Station before 7:00 A.M.? _____

12. If you leave Norfolk at 6:49 A.M., what time will you arrive at South Station? _____

13. Plimptonville is between which two towns? _____

B. Underline the correct answer to each question.

1. How long does it take to get from Franklin to Norfolk?
   a. 7 minutes   **b.** 3 minutes   **c.** 6 minutes

2. How many trains stop at all stations?
   a. 2   **b.** 5   **c.** 1

3. At which of these stations can you *not* buy train tickets?
   a. Franklin   **b.** Islington   **c.** Back Bay

4. Which of these stations should you avoid if you are in a wheelchair?
   a. Norwood Central   **b.** Endicott   **c.** Ruggles

5. You have an important breakfast meeting near South Station at 7:45 A.M. It takes about ten minutes to walk from the station to your meeting. What is the latest you could leave Walpole to be at your meeting on time?
   a. 6:05 A.M.   **b.** 6:35 A.M.   **c.** 6:55 A.M.

6. How long does it take to go from Forge Park to South Station on Train 700?
   a. 65 minutes   **b.** 55 minutes   **c.** one hour

7. Which town do you think is closest to Walpole?
   a. Franklin   **b.** Norfolk   **c.** Windsor Gardens

8. If you miss the first train out of Readville, how long will you have to wait for the next train?
   a. 29 minutes   **b.** 20 minutes   **c.** 5 minutes

9. How many trains stop at Norwood Depot?
   a. 4   **b.** 3   **c.** 6

10. Which train takes the least time to make the entire trip?
    a. 702   **b.** 704   **c.** 706

11. Which stations have the most trains leaving from them?
    a. Norwood Central and Dedham Corporate Ctr.
    b. Walpole and Dedham Corporate Ctr.
    c. Forge Park and Norwood Central

12. How often do the first three trains of the day run?
    a. every hour   **b.** every fifteen minutes   **c.** every half hour

Lesson 24

Conflict and Resolution

Reading a Literature Selection

▶ Background Information

In this story, 16-year-old Keema feels angry and confused after she moves to a new neighborhood and leaves her old friends behind. Keema and her family live in Harlem, which is a section of New York City located in northern Manhattan. Harlem was founded in 1658. Around 1910 many African Americans begin settling there. Soon it became one of the largest African American communities in the United States. After World War II, many Latin Americans moved to East Harlem, or Spanish Harlem.

In the 1920s, many African American artists, writers, and musicians came to Harlem to work and live. Some of the most famous writers from this period are Langston Hughes and Zora Neale Hurston. The jazz music, paintings, novels, and poetry created by these artists is now world famous. This period is called the Harlem Renaissance.

▶ Skill Focus

Characters are the people in a story. Usually one of the characters in a story faces a problem. The struggle to solve this problem is called the **conflict**.

There are three types of conflict in stories.

Conflict with Self A character in this type of conflict may have to struggle with his or her feelings. You might find this conflict in a story about a person who overcomes a fear of heights by climbing a mountain.

Conflict with Another Character In this type of conflict, one character may have a problem with another character. This conflict is often found in detective stories when a police officer is after a person who has broken the law.

Conflict with Nature A character in this type of conflict may come face-to-face with some danger or outside force over which he or she has no control. A story about people living in a town hit by an earthquake or a family lost at sea usually confronts this type of conflict.

Every character who faces a conflict tries to solve this problem. The solution to a story's problem, or conflict, is called the **resolution**. The resolution usually comes at the end of the story.

▶ Word Clues

Read the sentences below. Look for context clues that explain the underlined word.

As much as she missed her old neighborhood, Keema loved the bustle of this busy street. Everywhere she looked the street was bursting with activity.

If you do not know the meaning of the word *bustle*, the word *activity* in the next sentence can help you. The words *bustle* and *activity* are synonyms.

Use **synonym** context clues to find the meaning of the three underlined words in the selection.

▶ Strategy Tip

As you read "Something to Cheer About," pay special attention to the problem that Keema faces and how she solves it. What type of conflict does she face? What is the resolution?

Something to Cheer About

Nothing was going the way that 16-year-old Keema Watkins thought it would. After her family moved to Harlem in August, her life changed completely. "It's like my whole world turned upside down," Keema thought to herself. "One day I'm walking around my old neighborhood talking to my best friend, Marisa. And the next day, here I am. A new house, a new school, and no best friend."

Early one afternoon, Keema was walking down Amsterdam with her younger brother Jamal. It was a <u>crisp</u> October day. The cool, sharp air felt good after the hot, rainy summer. As much as she missed her old neighborhood, Keema loved the bustle of this busy street. Everywhere she looked the street was bursting with activity. Skaters on in-line skates whizzed by them. Shoppers crowded the busy stores. Music blared at Keema and Jamal from a dozen radios. Street <u>vendors</u> sold everything from hot dogs to CD's. One of these street sellers held out a steaming hot dog to

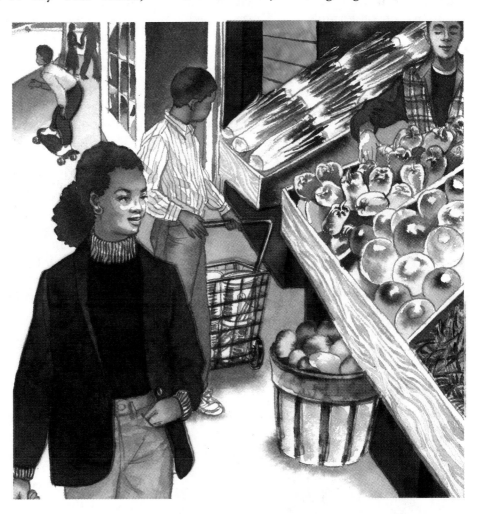

Jamal. "The best in New York," he said, grinning. "And there's no charge for the mustard, either."

But Jamal and Keema didn't have time to stop. They were looking for a hardware store so that they could buy house paint for their mother. This weekend, the whole family was going to paint the living room of their new house. The house was another thing that Keema couldn't quite get used to. It was great having a room to herself. In her old apartment, Keema had shared a bedroom with her mother. But fixing up an old house took a lot of time and work. Sometimes Keema wished that she just could shut her eyes and wake up in her old apartment again. More than anything, she missed her old life.

Jamal looked up at Keema. "Hey, stop daydreaming," he said. "If we don't find that hardware store, we are going to be in serious trouble. You know how important painting the house is to Mom." Jamal said, grinning.

Keema sighed and shook her head. "Tell me about it," she said. "Look, there's the hardware store. It's right next to the subway." As they crossed the street, a girl waved to Keema and called her name.

"Who's that?" Jamal asked, as they entered the hardware store.

"Maria Hernandez," Keema answered "She's in some of my classes."

Ten minutes later Keema paid for the paint while Jamal loaded it into their shopping cart.

"You two must be new to the neighborhood," the store manager said. "I've worked here almost forty years. I must know everyone in the area. Where do you live?"

"On West 13th Street—right near Sixth Avenue," Keema said without thinking.

The store manager looked surprised. "Then you sure are a long way from home," he said. "That's at the other end of the city."

Suddenly, Keema felt <u>embarrassed</u>. "I mean, we live on Hamilton Place," she said, looking uncomfortable. "We just picked up and moved here two months ago."

"Well, stop by again," the manager said as Keema and Jamal left the store. "Welcome to the neighborhood," he called after them.

"Hey, big sister," Jamal said, grinning. "I know you're not too happy about moving and

everything. But you at least can learn our new address. I think it's kind of a cool place to live."

Before Keema could answer, Maria Hernandez walked up to them. "I thought I saw you go into the hardware store," she said to Keema. "A couple of us are going in-line skating in the park this afternoon. Why don't you come along?"

Keema shook her head. "Thanks, but I promised my mom that I'd help her around the house today. Maybe some other time."

"Okay," Maria said. "See you in school on Monday."

As Maria walked away, Jamal turned to Keema. "She seems nice," he said.

Keema walked on without answering.

"Hey," Jamal yelled, as he tried to catch up with her. "What's wrong with you? At least help me with this shopping cart. This paint is heavy."

When Keema and Jamal carried the cans of paint into the living room, their mother was waiting for them. "Just in time," she said with a grin. "I've plastered every crack in this room. Now I can't wait to get my hands on a paint brush. Who's going to help me stir this paint?"

"Mom, I'm going to change into my old jeans," Keema said. "I'll be down in a minute." As Keema ran upstairs, Jamal looked at his mother and shrugged his shoulders.

The walls of Keema's bedroom were covered with pictures of her friends from her old high school. A banner that said "Washington Irving High School" hung above her bed. Keema looked at a photograph from last year's class party. She and Marisa grinned at the camera surrounded by all their friends. "It just isn't the same without you guys," Keema said to herself.

Keema was still thinking about her old friends on her way to school Monday morning. As she got off the crowded subway car and hurried down the street, she remembered what her mother had said to her at breakfast. "Honey, you have to give your new school a fair chance. You'll make new friends. Once you do, you'll like your new home as much as Jamal does. You'll see."

"Face it, Keema," she said to herself.

"Mom's right. So you had to move because of her great new job. What's the big deal? Lots of people move every day of the year. And that job was important to mom. So is owning a home. You really haven't given Park East a chance. Today is going to be different."

But when Keema walked into Park East High School, she didn't feel any different. All around her, groups of students were talking and laughing. Keema waved to a few students she knew on her way to the locker room. She didn't stop to talk to any of them. She was putting away her jacket when she saw Maria Hernandez.

"I'm glad I ran into you," Maria said. "I'm having a party this Friday night, and I'd love you to come. A lot of the kids from school will be there."

Keema wanted to say "yes." But the thought of going to a party with a bunch of kids she didn't know really scared her.

"Thanks for asking me, Maria," she said. "But this Friday, I'm seeing some friends from my old school. It's kind of a class party. They invited me weeks ago." Keema was trying so hard to sound natural that her words came out in a rush. It was all a lie and Maria knew it. Keema could tell by her look that Maria didn't believe her. And the strange thing was, Keema felt bad about lying to Maria.

On her way to her math class, Keema saw Maria walking down the hall ahead of her. For a second, Keema felt like telling her how she really felt; how she was the only one in her family who didn't like moving to a new neighborhood; how weird it was to walk to class without anyone to talk to or laugh with; and how she didn't really feel like Keema any more. "Forget it, Keema," she thought to herself. "Maria won't know what you're talking about."

That night, Keema and Jamal were washing the dinner dishes when the phone rang. It was Marisa.

As soon as she heard her friend's voice, Keema felt better. "Let's go to a movie this Friday," she said. "Maybe hang out with Lee and Josh afterward."

"I can't," Marisa said. "Don't you remember? We're going on a class trip this weekend. We won't be back until Sunday night."

Keema tried to hide the disappointment in her voice. "Oh sure," she said. "I forgot that it was this weekend. We went on a class trip the same time last year."

"This one won't be the same without you. We really miss you," Marisa said.

Keema smiled, but she felt like crying, too, and she wasn't sure why. "Let's do something when you guys get back," she said.

"Don't forget. We'll be seeing you in two weeks," Marisa said. "Our basketball team plays Park East at the end of this month. I'll save a seat for you on our side of the court."

For the next two weeks, Keema kept thinking about what her "side of the court" really was. She missed Marisa and her friends from her old high school. Still, Keema was starting to feel more at home in her new school.

The day before the big basketball game, Keema walked to English class with Maria. They were laughing about a really bad movie that they both had seen. "You're the only person who likes bad movies as much as I do," Keema said.

"I really got into them when I transferred to Park East last spring," Maria said.

"I thought you had been here since ninth grade," Keema said.

Maria shook her head. "Nope. I'm a newcomer, just like you. So, I know what it's like leaving your old friends behind," she said. Then she and Keema walked into English class together.

That Friday night, the gym was filled with students from Park East and Washington Irving. When Keema and Jamal walked into the gym, she heard Marisa call her name. The two friends hugged.

"I have so much to tell you," Keema said. "I don't know where to begin."

Marisa pointed to an empty seat beside her. "Come sit with us."

Keema looked across the court. She could see Maria and her new friends waving to her. Then she turned back to Marisa. "You know how much you all mean to me. But tonight, I want to cheer for Park East. It's where I belong now." Then she and Jamal sat down next to Maria.

The crowd roared as the basketball players took their places on the court. Keema and Jamal started cheering, too. For the first time in a long time, she had something to cheer about.

1. How do Keema and Jamal feel about moving to their new neighborhood?

   _____

   _____

2. What happens after Maria sees Keema and Jamal come out of the hardware store?

   _____

   _____

3. Why did Keema and Jamal move to Harlem?

   _____

   _____

4. How does Keema react when she arrives at school on Monday?

   _____

   _____

5. Why doesn't Keema accept Maria's invitation to her party?

   _____

   _____

6. Why can't Marisa go to the movies with Keema?

   _____

   _____

7. In what ways are Keema and Maria alike?

   _____

   _____

8. What is the resolution of the conflict?

   _____

   _____

9. Decide if each statement is true or false. Write true or false on the lines provided.

   a. When the air feels crisp, the temperature is cool and dry.

      _____

   b. A vendor is someone who sings and dances.

      _____

   c. If a person feels embarrassed, he or she is very self-confident.

      _____

1. Why do you think Keema gives the wrong address when the store manager asks her where she lives?

   _____

   _____

   _____

2. Why do you think Keema walks away from Jamal after he says that Maria Hernandez seems nice?

   _____

   _____

3. Why do you think Keema and her brother Jamal react so differently to the move to a new neighborhood?

   _____

   _____

   _____

4. Why do you think Keema feels bad about lying to Maria?

   _____

   _____

5. Why do you think Keema feels like crying when she talks to Marisa on the phone?

_____

_____

_____

6. How do you think Maria feels when Keema turns down her invitation to go in-line skating and to attend her party?

_____

_____

_____

SKILL FOCUS

Think about the conflict that Keema Watkins faces and how she solves it. Write your answers on the lines below.

1. Reread the three kinds of conflict described on page 62. What kind of conflict does Keema Watkins face?

_____

_____

2. What causes this conflict?

_____

_____

3. How does Keema feel about this conflict?

_____

_____

4. How is this conflict resolved?

_____

_____

5. What does Keema learn from her experience?

_____

_____

6. How do you think Keema will change as a result of this experience?

_____

_____

▶ **Real Life Connections** Put yourself in Keema's shoes. Describe what you would do at the basketball game. Which side would you sit on?

Comparing and Contrasting

___ Reading a Social Studies Selection ___

▶ Background Information

Do you like animals? Have you ever considered becoming an animal doctor? It doesn't matter whether you live in the city or in the country. Veterinarians are needed in both places. But don't expect the job to be the same! The jobs of city vets and country vets are alike in some ways, but quite different in others.

The selection you are about to read describes the work of two veterinarians, one a country vet and one a city vet.

▶ Skill Focus

When reading a textbook, you will often need to compare two or more people, places, or events. To **compare** is to point out what is the same. To make a comparison, look for similarities. To **contrast** is to point out what is different. To find contrasts, look for differences. Sometimes people, places, or events are both similar and different at the same time.

There are two ways writers give information when comparing and contrasting two topics. The first way is to tell several details about one topic and then tell details about the other. The information about each topic is usually given in separate paragraphs.

Another way is to cover two topics point by point, detail by detail. Information that compares or contrasts details about both topics is given in the same paragraph. When you read this type of paragraph, you have to sort out the details that belong to each topic. Looking for details will help when comparing and contrasting.

As you read "City Vets, Country Vets," try to determine which method of comparing and contrasting the author used.

▶ Word Clues

Read the sentence below. Look for context clues that explain the underlined word.

Dr. Catherine Ling, an underline vet, sometimes sees in her city practice such unusual patients as chameleons, parrots, ferrets, and snakes.

If you don't know the meaning of the word *urban*, the word *city* in the same sentence will help you. The words *city* and *urban* are synonyms. Urban areas are cities.

Context clues can come before or after the unknown word. When you come across a word that you don't know, be sure to look for the context clues in the sentence before and after the word, as well as in the same sentence.

Use **synonym** context clues to find the meaning of the three underlined words in the selection.

▶ Strategy Tip

In "City Vets, Country Vets," the lives and practices of a city vet and country vet are compared and contrasted on the basis of three points: the work that they do, the places where they work, and their specialities.

As you read each section, you will find information comparing the two topics—city vets and country vets. Knowing how information is organized will help you find the details about each topic.

City Vets, Country Vets

1. Veterinarians weren't always around. In fact, the first veterinary schools weren't started until the late 1700s. Before that time, animals were cared for by the people who worked with them—shepherds, blacksmiths, farmers, stable hands, and others. These people depended on their experience and sometimes folk wisdom, rather than science, to treat their animals. The first trained veterinarians generally treated only large animals, such as cows, horses, sheep, goats, and pigs. These animals were very important in a farm-based economy. Vets who specialized in treating small animals, mainly pets, were unheard of at that time. But then cities grew, and society and the economy changed. More people started owning pets. Gradually, more and more veterinarians began setting up small-animal practices.

The Work Vets Do

2. Today Dr. Wendell Jordan and veterinarians like him—those who work in small towns and rural areas—usually have a mixed practice. These country vets still treat horses and <u>livestock</u>, such as dairy cows and pigs, but they also treat wildlife and pets. Dr. Jordan usually spends the morning in his office taking care of small animals that are brought in. Often these are pet cats and dogs that need checkups, shots, or medicine. That part of his practice is like a city vet's. Sometimes, however, a small patient turns out to be a wild animal like an injured fawn. That's not to say that a city vet's practice is dull! People living in cities often have exotic pets. Dr. Catherine Ling, an urban vet, sometimes sees in her city practice such unusual patients as chameleons, parrots, ferrets, and snakes.

3. Dr. Jordan's practice differs from Dr. Ling's mainly in that he spends a good part of the day traveling around to ranches, farms, and stables. He must often treat more than one animal at a time, something city vets don't usually do. For example, he must test or treat a whole herd of dairy cows to prevent the spread of disease. The treatment of entire herds is important because farmers and ranchers depend on the health of their livestock to make a living. Diseases among livestock can wipe out not only a farmer's own animals but also those on neighboring farms. Some of these diseases, such as brucellosis, can also affect humans. Both country vets and city vets help prevent the spread of animal diseases to people.

4. An important part of every veterinarian's practice is emergency care for badly injured or very sick animals. The need for emergency care is especially true for country vets, because farmers and ranchers often treat their own animals. Sometimes, farmers and ranchers call Dr. Jordan only when an animal is quite sick, limiting his ability to treat the animal successfully. By contrast, pet owners in the city generally don't treat their own animals or wait until the animal is very sick. Dr. Ling is therefore likely to spend much of her day in routine health care. Such tasks include

regularly cleaning teeth and ears and testing for heartworms.

Where Vets Work

5. Like many other city veterinarians, Dr. Ling works with a team of vets in a clinic. Generally large animal clinics and hospitals are equipped like human hospitals. Most anything the vets need to do—whether taking X rays of broken bones, performing eye surgery, or running laboratory tests—can be done where they work. Working in teams is helpful because the vets can see a greater number and variety of patients. They can then share valuable information.

✔ 6. The workplace is quite different for a country vet. Once Dr. Jordan leaves his office, his examining room or operating room may be a pasture or a barn stall. Equipment has to be <u>portable</u>, small enough to be carried in a truck or van. Unlike Dr. Ling, he does not have with him a laboratory that can do tests. He must depend on his own knowledge and experience to determine what a problem is. If he needs special equipment or must do complicated surgery, then Dr. Jordan must arrange to use a clinic. And when his visits are done, his workday is not necessarily over. Country vets are often "on call" and receive phone calls day and night. City vets like Dr. Ling, on the other hand, usually take turns covering emergencies after office hours.

The Specialists

✔ 7. Vets like Dr. Jordan and Dr. Ling have a general practice. They see all kinds of animals and treat all kinds of problems. There are country and city vets, however, who have a special practice. Some country vets, for instance, specialize in treating horses. These <u>equine</u> vets keep quite busy vaccinating their patients, treating them for worms, and helping them when they give birth. Similarly, some city vets specialize in treating cats or birds. Others may specialize in an area of medicine such as dermatology (for skin problems), dentistry, and ophthalmology (for eye problems). Because a vet may be the only specialist in the city, he or she may travel from one clinic to another to see patients.

RECALLING FACTS

1. Before there were trained veterinarians, who took care of farm animals?

_____

_____

2. Why did the first veterinarians treat only large animals?

_____

_____

3. Why did veterinarians begin to set up small-animal practices?

_____

_____

4. How do both country vets and city vets help human beings?

_____

_____

5. List one area in which a city vet's practice differs from a country vet's practice.

_____

_____

_____

6. Two paragraphs have check marks before them. Reread each one and underline the sentence that states the main idea.

7. Underline the word that best completes each sentence.

   a. A country vet treats dairy cows, pigs, and other _____.

      herds   wildlife   livestock

   b. Some vets might specialize in one type of animal, such as horses. These

   _____ vets treat injuries and diseases that affect only horses.

      equine   bovine   feline

   c. A country vet's equipment has to be

   _____, or easy to carry.

      portable   exotic   valuable

INTERPRETING FACTS

---

1. Circle the letter of the statement that best expresses the main idea of the whole selection.

   a. Country vets must treat a greater variety of animals than city vets.

   b. The jobs of city vets and country vets are alike in some ways, but quite different in others.

   c. The work of veterinarians has changed greatly since the late 1700s.

2. Put a check mark before each statement that can be supported with a fact from the selection.

   _____ People's attitudes about pets have changed greatly since veterinarians first began to practice.

   _____ Farmers and ranchers don't value a veterinarian's skill as much as city pet owners do.

   _____ Country vets need more training than city vets.

   _____ City vets can sometimes treat problems faster than country vets.

3. What important job does a country vet have that a city vet doesn't?

   _____

   _____

   _____

4. Name one advantage that a city vet has over a country vet.

   _____

   _____

   _____

   _____

SKILL FOCUS

Country vets and city vets have jobs that are alike in some ways and different in others. Use the similarities and differences between them to answer the following questions.

1. Reread paragraphs 2–4 under the heading "The Work They Do." Notice that each paragraph compares and contrasts the work of country vets and city vets. List one similarity and one difference mentioned in each paragraph.

Paragraph 2:

Alike: _____

Different: _____

Paragraph 3:

Alike: _____

_____

Different: _____

_____

Paragraph 4:

Alike: _____

_____

Different: _____

_____

2. Reread paragraphs 5 and 6 under the heading "Where They Work." On the lines below, summarize the differences in the ways in which city vets and country vets work.

City Vets: _____

_____

Country Vets: _____

_____

3. Reread the text under the last heading, "The Specialists." What do some country vets and some city vets have in common?

_____

_____

4. Look at the chart below. Decide whether each detail in the first column describes a city vet, a country vet, or both. Then put a check mark under the appropriate heads.

	City Vet	Country Vet
Treats livestock		
Treats pets		
Helps prevent spread of disease		
Often does routine work like cleaning teeth		
Often travels		
May treat only a particular kind of animal		

▶ **Real Life Connections** If possible, conduct an interview with a local veterinarian. How is the veterinarian the same as or different from Dr. Ling and Dr. Jordan?

Cause and Effect

Reading a Science Selection

▶ Background Information

A wide variety of food crops is grown on farms in the United States. Because of the different climates, some states are better than others for growing a particular food crop. In Florida, for example, the climate is ideal for oranges. On the other hand, in Nebraska, the climate is better for corn.

The variety of food crops grown in the United States farming industry is very important. Without farms to grow different fruits and vegetables, people couldn't get the foods that they need to stay healthy.

A healthy diet is one that includes many different kinds of foods. For instance, oranges provide a great deal of Vitamin C, but do not have much Vitamin D. In order to balance your vitamin intake, you should see which foods have which vitamins and plan your meals accordingly.

▶ Skill Focus

The cause of something is the reason it happens. The effect is what happens as a result of the cause. Think about **causes** and their **effects** as you read "Vitamins and Other Nutrients." For example, if a person is angry, he or she might slam a door. The cause is anger. The effect is the slamming of a door. Sometimes it is very clear what effect a certain cause will have. Sometimes it is not so clear. Look for words, such as *cause, effect, because, so, result, that is why*. They often signal cause and effect. Read the following sentences.

> Sue got a good grade in English so she was happy.
>
> Sue was happy *because* she got a good grade in English.

In the first sentence, the cause is given first. In the second sentence, the effect is given first.

Sometimes you need to read more than one sentence to find the cause and effect. Read the following sentences.

> Carlos was quite unhappy. He failed his math test.
>
> Carlos failed his math test. As a *result*, he was quite unhappy.

In the first pair of sentences, the effect is given first. In the second, the cause is given first. In both, the effect is that Carlos was unhappy.

▶ Word Clues

Read the sentences below. Look for context clues that explain the underlined word.

> Nutrients are <u>substances</u> that the body needs to stay healthy. These materials give the body energy and help it to grow and to repair itself.

If you do not know the meaning of the word *substances*, the word *materials* in the next sentence can help you. The words *substances* and *materials* are synonyms. Substances are materials.

Use **synonym** context clues to find the meaning of the three underlined words in the selection.

▶ Strategy Tip

Look for causes and effects as you read "Vitamins and Other Nutrients." Remember that a cause is the reason something happens. An effect is what happens as a result of a cause. Also remember to look for signal words.

Vitamins and Other Nutrients

Nutrients (NOO tree ənts) are substances that the body needs to stay healthy. These materials give the body energy and help it to grow and to repair itself. A balanced diet provides all the nutrients that the body needs. A balanced diet helps a person stay in good health. The food pyramid is shown in Figure 1 below. Eating the number of suggested servings from each of the food groups will provide a balanced diet.

✔ Vitamins, **organic** (or GAN ik) substances found in foods, help control the body's functions. An organic substance is something that is, or once was, part of a plant or an animal. Vitamins are nutrients, but they do not provide energy by themselves. They work with other nutrients to regulate the body's functions. The body cannot work without them.

Scientists have identified 13 vitamins. Vitamins are needed only in tiny amounts, but the lack of some vitamins can cause diseases. A Scottish doctor, James Lind, was one of the first to suggest that the lack of certain nutrients could cause illnesses. The word *vitamine* was first used in 1912 by a Polish scientist named Casimir Funk.

Today scientists put vitamins into two main groups: water-soluble and fat-soluble. Water-soluble vitamins dissolve, or melt, in water. Fat-soluble vitamins dissolve, or melt, in fat. The water-soluble vitamins are B_1, which is also called **thiamin** (THY ə meen); B_2, which is also called **riboflavin** (RY bə flay vin); **niacin** (NY ə sin); B_6, also called **pyridoxine** (pir ə DOK seen); **pantothenic** (pan tə THEN ik) acid; B_{12}, **biotin** (BY ə tin); C, which is also called **ascorbic** (ə SKOR bik) **acid**; and **folic** (FOH lik) **acid**. The fat-soluble vitamins are A, D, E, and K.

The body needs specific amounts of certain vitamins for good health. Scientists have discovered what these certain amounts are. They have figured out a Recommended Dietary Allowance, or RDA, for most vitamins. If a person has a **deficiency** (di FISH ən see), or lack, of these vitamins, the result can be a deficiency disease. Figure 2 shows the effects of certain vitamin deficiencies.

Fats, Oils, Sweets
USE SPARINGLY

Milk, Yogurt,
Cheese Group
2–3 SERVINGS

Meat, Poultry, Fish,
Dry beans, Eggs,
Nut Group
2–3 SERVINGS

Vegetable
Group
3–5 SERVINGS

Fruit Group
2–4 SERVINGS

Bread, Cereal,
Rice, Pasta
Group
6–11
SERVINGS

Figure 1. The suggested number of servings from each of the food groups should be eaten daily.

Vitamin	Disease Caused by Deficiency	Symptoms	Foods Containing Vitamin
B_1 (thiamin)	beriberi	stiffness and pain in legs; weakness	pork, green vegetables, yeast, nuts
niacin	pellagra	nervousness; indigestion	beef, liver, yeast, whole wheat bread
C (ascorbic acid)	scurvy	sore, bleeding gums; bruising	oranges, lemons, grapefruit, melon, raw cabbage, tomatoes
D	rickets	soft, crooked bones in young children	enriched milk, fish oils

Figure 2. Deficiency diseases are caused by a lack of certain vitamins.

The body can make some vitamins. When sunlight shines on the skin, the body produces vitamin D. Some vitamins cannot be made or stored in the body. Vitamin C is an example. If a person doesn't take in any vitamin C over a period of time, a deficiency can develop in the body.

Some vitamins cannot be made or stored in the body. Vitamin C is an example.

Vitamins are now added to many foods so that people take in more vitamins. For example, vitamin D is added to milk. Because of enriched foods, deficiency diseases are not as common today as they once were.

Many people also take vitamin pills. Most vitamin pills contain **synthetic** (sin THET ik) vitamins. Synthetic vitamins are made in laboratories. Natural vitamins are found in foods. The vitamins that are added to enriched foods are also synthetic.

In the future, scientists may discover several new vitamins. New uses may also be discovered for the known vitamins. Scientists are experimenting to find out if vitamins can cure or prevent diseases like cancer and heart disease. It may be that vitamins are even more important than we think.

RECALLING FACTS

1. What are nutrients?

_____

_____

2. What is an organic substance?

_____

_____

3. How do vitamins work in the body?

_____

_____

4. Who are two scientists who worked with vitamins?

_____

5. What is a deficiency?

_____

6. What are synthetic vitamins?

_____

7. What are natural vitamins?

_____

Lesson 26 *Identifying cause and effect* 75

8. Reread the paragraph in the selection that has a check mark next to it. Underline the sentence that has the main idea.

9. What are the two main groups into which scientists classify vitamins?

_____

_____

10. A person who has scurvy might need more foods from which food group?

_____

_____

11. A person who has rickets might need more foods from which two groups?

_____

_____

_____

12. A person should have up to 11 servings daily from which food group?

_____

_____

13. Which vitamin can the body make when sunlight shines on the skin?

_____

14. If a person is suffering from beriberi, what vitamin does that person need?

_____

_____

15. A deficiency of niacin can cause which disease?

_____

_____

16. A child with soft, crooked bones might need which vitamin?

_____

_____

17. Underline the word that correctly completes each sentence.

a. Chicken pox and mumps are kinds of childhood _____.

      vitamins   **nutrients**   **diseases**

b. Turn the temperature knob to _____ the heater.

      regulate   **dissolve**   **melt**

c. Thiamin is a _____ type of water-soluble vitamin.

      deficiency   **specific**   **healthy**

INTERPRETING FACTS

1. On the lines next to each food, write the food group to which it belongs.

a. candy _____

b. carrots _____

c. noodles _____

d. hamburger _____

e. oranges _____

2. List the foods that you would include for a balanced meal. Be sure to list foods from the food pyramid. _____

_____

3. Long ago, English sailors developed scurvy while on long overseas trips. Why do you think they developed this disease?

_____

_____

_____

_____

SKILL FOCUS

Draw a line to match each cause with its effect.

Causes	*Effects*
1. sun shining on person's skin	a. good health
2. vitamin deficiencies	b. important discoveries
3. enriched foods	c. vitamin D
4. a balanced diet	d. fewer people with deficiency diseases
5. scientists conducting experiments	e. deficiency diseases

Write a sentence that states each cause and effect that you matched above. Start the first three sentences with the cause, the remaining two with the effect. Be sure to use signal words.

1. _____

_____

2. _____

_____

3. _____

_____

4. _____

_____

5. _____

_____

▶ **Real Life Connections** Based on what you know about the food pyramid, plan a healthful diet for yourself for one day. Be realistic. Be sure to include foods that you would enjoy eating.

Reading a Thermometer

Reading a Mathematics Selection

▶ Background Information

Temperature, or the amount of heat in a substance, is measured by a thermometer. They are used for measuring both indoor and outdoor air temperatures. They are also used to measure the cooking temperatures of various foods. We rely on thermometers to tell us what kind of clothes are appropriate for any given day. We also use thermometers to measure our body temperature. For instance, if your body temperature is 101° F, or 101 degrees Fahrenheit, you should probably stay home from school.

Today there are three temperature systems in use— **Fahrenheit** (FER ən hyt), **Celsius** (SEL see əs), and **Kelvin** (KEL vən). In "Reading a Thermometer," you will learn more about Fahrenheit and Celsius. Kelvin is the system that scientists use. (If you would like to learn more about the Kelvin system, ask your science teacher.)

Fahrenheit is the system most widely used in the United States. When someone tells you that it is 95° F, they are using the Fahrenheit system.

The Fahrenheit system was developed by Gabriel Daniel Fahrenheit in 1714. Fahrenheit used mercury (the silver liquid that is in thermometers). Until that point, alcohol was used in thermometers.

Most of the rest of the world uses Celsius. Also called Centigrade (SEN tə grayd), this system was developed by Anders Celsius in 1742. While the Celsius system also uses mercury, its readings are vastly different from those of the Fahrenheit system.

In this selection, you will learn how to read both the Fahrenheit and Celsius systems. Knowing the basics of both systems is important because they are still widely used systems for measuring temperatures.

▶ Skill Focus

Learning to read a thermometer is an important skill. It is necessary for people to record a variety of temperatures in many different professions. For example, weather forecasters report the air temperature in their forecasts. Nurses take a patient's body temperature to measure the person's health.

▶ Word Clues

When reading the following selection, look for these important words: *Fahrenheit, Celsius, centigrade, degrees.* They will help you understand more about temperature and thermometers.

▶ Strategy Tip

When reading about mathematics or science, it is often necessary to refer to the diagrams. Use the text and diagrams until you understand the ideas and concepts being explained. Also look for special words that refer to temperature.

Reading a Thermometer

Look at Figure 1 below. It shows a type of thermometer found in many homes in the United States. Notice that the colored liquid is at the line marked 68. The symbol ° stands for the word *degree*. The letter *F* stands for the word *Fahrenheit*. The temperature shown on the Fahrenheit thermometer in Figure 1 is written as 68°F.

As the air gets warmer, the colored liquid in the thermometer goes up, or rises. This upward movement shows that the temperature is increasing, or rising.

The invention of the thermometer is attributed to Galileo. The first sealed thermometer was produced by the German physicist Daniel Gabriel Fahrenheit in 1714.

As the air becomes cooler, the liquid goes down, or drops. This downward movement shows that the temperature is decreasing, or dropping.

Notice that the degree lines are numbered above and below zero. There are two degree lines numbered 10 and two numbered 20. The numbers below zero are marked with a minus sign. When speaking of a temperature that is less than zero, the following wording is used: *minus* 10 degrees Fahrenheit, or 10 degrees *below zero* on the Fahrenheit scale.

Figure 1. The Fahrenheit thermometer is still used in the United States.

Figure 2. The Celsius thermometer is used in most parts of the world.

✔ The Celsius thermometer works in the same way, but different numbers are used to show the same degree of heat. On the Celsius scale, 0° is used to show the temperature at which water freezes. On the Fahrenheit scale, 32° is used to show the temperature at which water freezes. On the Celsius scale, 100° is used to show the temperature at which water boils. On the Fahrenheit scale, 212° is used to show the temperature at which water boils.

Now look at Figure 2 on page 79. It shows a Celsius, or centigrade, thermometer. The degrees are called Celsius, or centigrade. The letter C stands for *Celsius*. Notice that 0°C is the same as 32°F. In Figures 1 and 2, each of the small lines stands for two degrees. The markings on the four thermometers shown on page 81 are also in two degree increments.

RECALLING FACTS

1. Most thermometers are numbered above zero and _____ zero.

2. The liquid in both Fahrenheit and Celsius thermometers _____ when the air gets warmer.

3. The liquid _____ when the air gets cooler.

4. Reread the paragraph in "Reading a Thermometer" that has a check mark next to it. Underline the sentence that has the main idea.

INTERPRETING FACTS

1. Explain in your own words how the liquid in a thermometer shows a higher temperature.

_____

_____

_____

_____

2. Explain in your own words how the liquid in a thermometer shows a lower temperature.

_____

_____

_____

_____

SKILL FOCUS

1. What is the temperature shown on Thermometer 1 on page 81? _____

2. If the temperature dropped to 20°F below zero, would this be colder than or warmer than 10°F above zero? _____

3. Thermometer 2 on page 81 shows 212°F. How many degrees above the freezing point of water is its boiling point? _____

4. In Thermometer 3 below, the temperature is shown as 98°F. This is close to the usual temperature of our bodies. How many degrees above the usual room temperature (70°F) is the usual body temperature? _____

5. If the temperature of the water at the beach in the summer is 67°F, how much cooler is the water than a person's body? _____

6. Thermometer 3 below shows your normal body temperature on a Fahrenheit scale. Thermometer 4 shows it on the Celsius scale. What is the normal body temperature in Celsius degrees? _____

7. Which is colder, 10°F or 10°C? _____

8. Which is colder, –25°F or 7°C? _____

9. What is the freezing point of water on the Celsius scale? _____

10. What is the boiling point of water on the Celsius scale? _____

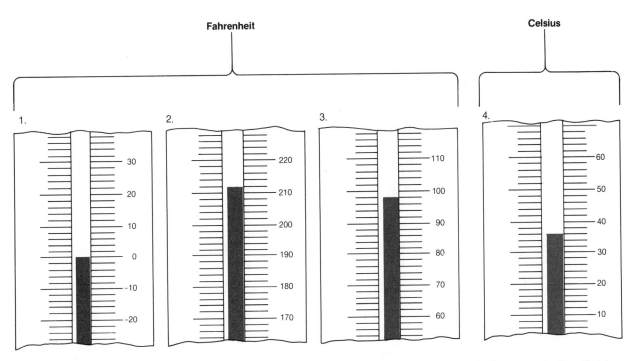

Thermometers 1, 2, and 3 show parts of a Fahrenheit thermometer. Thermometer 4 shows part of a Celsius thermometer.

▶ **Real Life Connections** What is today's temperature outside?

_____ on a Fahrenheit scale   _____ on a Celsius scale

What is today's temperature inside your classroom or house?

_____ on a Fahrenheit scale   _____ on a Celsius scale

Lesson 28

r-Controlled Vowel Sounds

Vowels can have sounds in addition to their long and short sounds. If the letter *r* comes after a vowel, the *r* controls the sound of the vowel. The sounds of *ar, er, ir, or,* and *ur* are called **r-controlled vowel sounds.**

Say the word pairs below, listening to each vowel sound. Answer the questions that follow.

cap	hem	sit	fog	fun
car	her	sir	for	fur

1. Is the sound of the vowel in the top word of each pair long or short? _____

2. Does the vowel in the bottom word of each pair have a different sound? _____

3. What letter follows the vowel in the bottom word of each pair? _____

Say the words in the list after each number below. Listen to the vowel sound in each word. Answer each question with *yes* or *no*. Then complete the guide below.

1. bar
   star
   farm
   Does the *a* in these words have a sound that is different from either long *a* or short *a*? ____

2. dare
   hare
   share
   Does the *a* in these words have a sound that is different from either long *a* or short *a*? ____

3. herd
   term
   stern
   Does the *e* in these words have a sound that is different from either long *e* or short *e*? ____

4. shirt
   bird
   third
   Does the *i* in these words have a sound that is different from either long *i* or short *i*? ____

5. for
   born
   storm
   Does the *o* in these words have a sound that is different from either long *o* or short *o*? ____

6. burn
   hurt
   curve
   Does the *u* in these words have a sound that is different from either long *u* or short *u*? ____

> **Guide 4a:** When the vowel in a one-vowel word is followed by _____, the sound of the vowel is usually changed by the _____, and the sound of the vowel is neither short nor long.

Listen to the sound of *e, i,* and *u* in the following words. Then complete the guide below.

jerk	term	dirt	mirth	fur	curl
perk	her	fir	shirk	burn	urn

> **Guide 4b:** When the vowels *e, i,* and u are followed by _____, all three vowels usually have the _____ sound.

82 Lesson 28 *Recognizing r-controlled vowel sounds*

Prefixes, Suffixes, and Root Words

A **prefix** is a word part that is added to the beginning of a root word. A **suffix** is a word part that is added to the end of a root word. Both prefixes and suffixes change the meaning of a root word.

Some common prefixes and suffixes with their meanings are listed below. Study them before doing the exercises that follow.

Prefix	Meaning	Suffix	Meaning
in	in, toward	en	made of, to become
pre	before	er	one who does
re	again, or do over	ful	full of
un	not, or the opposite of	ly	like in appearance or manner
		ness	quality or state of

Choose one of the listed prefixes to add to the beginning of each root word below. Write the prefix on the line to the left of the root word. Make the new word mean the same thing as the phrase to the right of the word.

1. _____ do   do again
2. _____ pay   pay before
3. _____ happy   not happy
4. _____ game   before the game
5. _____ paint   paint again
6. _____ tie   not tied

7. _____ wrap   wrap again
8. _____ lock   not locked
9. _____ start   start again
10. _____ war   before the war
11. _____ make   make again
12. _____ cook   cook before

Choose one of the listed suffixes above to add to the end of each root word below. Write the suffix on the line to the right of the root word. Make the new word mean the same thing as the phrase to the right of the word.

1. teach _____   one who teaches
2. kind _____   in a kind way
3. truth _____   full of truth
4. loud _____   state of being loud
5. polite _____   quality of being polite
6. hope _____   full of hope

8. build _____   one who builds
9. dark _____   to become dark
10. slow _____   in a slow way
11. paint _____   one who paints
12. read _____   one who reads
13. joy _____   full of joy

Lesson 30

Syllables

A **syllable** is a word or part of a word. Each part of a word in which you can hear a vowel sound is a syllable.

A. Look at the following pictures and say their names. Listen for the number of vowel sounds that you hear in each one. Write 1 or 2 on the line after each picture to show the number of vowel sounds in its name.

dog _____

camel _____

monkey _____

giraffe _____

fish _____

tiger _____

B. Write the number of vowel letters that you see in each word below. Then read each word and write the number of vowel sounds that you hear.

	Vowel Letters	Vowel Sounds			Vowel Letters	Vowel Sounds
skin	____	____		darkness	____	____
jacket	____	____		pencil	____	____
pelt	____	____		trap	____	____

Write the correct word in the sentence below.

The number of vowel sounds that you hear tells you the number of _____ a word has.

You have learned that *e* is usually silent when it comes at the end of a word that has only one other vowel, such as *mile* or *same*. A final silent *e* is not counted as a vowel sound in deciding how many syllables are in a word.

What about a word in which two vowels are together, such as *boat* or *reach*? Would you count each one of these vowels as a vowel sound?

Write the correct numbers on the lines.

	Vowels	Sounded Vowels	Silent Vowels	Syllables		Vowels	Sounded Vowels	Silent Vowels	Syllables
race	____	____	____	____	wait	____	____	____	____
trade	____	____	____	____	coast	____	____	____	____
wise	____	____	____	____	team	____	____	____	____

Write the correct word in the sentence below.

The only vowel that affects the number of syllables is the one that is _____.

Lesson 31

Syllables

To help you pronounce compound words that you don't know, divide the words into syllables. Then you can pronounce each syllable until you can say the whole word. There are several ways of deciding how a word should be divided.

Compound Words

One of the easiest guides to use in dividing words is the one that is used with compound words. Since a compound word is made up of two words, it must have at least two syllables. Always divide a compound word into syllables by separating it between the two smaller words first.

rowboat   row boat

Read each of the following compound words. Divide the word into syllables by writing each of the two smaller words separately on the line to the right of the compound word.

1. snowflake _____   5. flashlight _____   9. campfire _____

2. sunlight _____   6. cupboard _____   10. fishhook _____

3. daytime _____   7. sandstorm _____   11. popcorn _____

4. snowshoe _____   8. classroom _____   12. spearhead _____

Fill in the words necessary to complete the following guide.

> **Guide 1:** A compound word is divided into _____ between the _____ smaller words.

Words with Double Consonants

Another guide that you may use is for words with double consonants. In such words, divide the word into syllables between the two consonants.

hammer   ham mer

Underline the double consonants in each of the following two-syllable words. Then divide each word into syllables between the double consonants. Write each syllable separately on the line to the right of each word.

1. gallon _____   6. summer _____   11. bottom _____

2. mammal _____   7. suppose _____   12. puppy _____

3. happen _____   8. appear _____   13. fellow _____

4. village _____   9. lettuce _____   14. parrot _____

5. letter _____   10. flutter _____   15. rabbit _____

Fill in the words necessary to complete the following guide.

> **Guide 2:** A word that has a _____ consonant is divided into syllables between the _____ consonants.

Comparing Food Labels

When shopping at a supermarket for a product, such as applesauce, you will notice that several brands are available. How do you know which kind to buy? The best thing to do is to compare the **labels** on the jars.

The information on food labels tells you about the products. Every food label identifies the weight of the product in ounces or quarts and in grams or liters. Federal law requires food companies to list ingredients on every food label. The ingredients show exactly what the product is made of. They are generally listed in order from the largest amount to the smallest amount. A food label also provides nutrition facts that note how many servings are in the container and the number of calories per serving. The percent daily value is also listed for nutrients most closely related to health, based on a 2,000-calorie diet.

Food labels provide facts about weight, ingredients, and nutrition. Be aware, however, of other information provided on a label to try to convince you to buy the product. Such information represents the opinion of the company that sells the product and may or may not be true.

Study the labels on the jar of Mighty Apple applesauce and Uncle Mort's applesauce.

Use the information on the labels to complete each sentence.

1. The applesauce made in Iowa is _____.

2. Each jar of Uncle Mort's applesauce contains _____ calories.

3. The larger jar of applesauce is called _____.

4. According to the label, you'll love _____.

5. Corn syrup and _____ are added to Mighty Apple applesauce to make it sweeter.

6. The two ingredients common to both brands of applesauce are _____.

7. The applesauce that adds vitamin C to retain color and flavor is _____.

8. The most of any one ingredient used in both kinds of applesauce is _____.

9. The ingredient used in the least amount in Uncle Mort's applesauce is _____.

10. The ingredient used in the least amount in Mighty Apple applesauce is _____.

11. The nutrient in Uncle Mort's applesauce with the highest percent daily value is

_____.

12. Someone on a diet would be better off eating _____ applesauce

because _____.

13. There are _____ servings in a _____ -ounce jar of Uncle Mort's applesauce.

14. There are _____ servings in a _____ -ounce jar of Mighty Apple applesauce.

15. A $7\frac{1}{2}$ -ounce jar of Uncle Mort's applesauce costs $.79. A 15-ounce jar of Mighty Apple applesauce costs $1.55. Which applesauce is less expensive per serving? If four servings of Mighty Apple applesauce cost $1.55, then one serving would cost _____ cents.

One serving of Uncle Mort's applesauce would cost _____ . So _____ applesauce is less expensive.

16. The applesauce that offers a money-back guarantee is _____.

17. The money-back guarantee means that if you are dissatisfied with the product,

_____ will return the money you paid for the applesauce.

18. You know that no preservatives or artificial colorings are added to Uncle Mort's

applesauce because the label states that this applesauce is _____.

19. The name Uncle Mort's applesauce may have been created to make the buyer think that

_____.

20. The company that manufactures Uncle Mort's applesauce is _____.

21. The metric weight of Mighty Apple applesauce is _____.

22. What is the percent daily value of protein in one serving of Uncle Mort's applesauce?

_____

23. If you were going to purchase one of these two brands of applesauce, you would buy

_____ because _____.

Lesson 33 _____

Theme

Reading a Literature Selection _____

▶ **Background Information**

Have you ever had something to do that you had to do all by yourself? Was it because of a contest? Was it just because you wanted to be proud of doing something alone?

In "Hopping Mad!" Nancy is rebuilding a car. Her dad and one of her friends are mechanics. How can she resist their help?

▶ **Skill Focus**

Theme is the meaning or message in a story. It also reflects the purpose, or reason, that the author had for writing the story. The theme is usually a message about people or about life in general. The theme in many stories is stated directly. Usually one of the characters will state the theme.

However, most writers do not directly tell the theme of their stories. Instead, the reader has to infer, or figure out, the theme. In stories in which you must figure out the theme, you have to look at the whole story and think about what the author is trying to tell you.

Often the title of a story tells in very few words what the story is about. Many times, the title is a clue to a story's theme. Always pay attention to the titles of the stories that you read.

The questions below will help you figure out the theme of a story.

1. What does the title of the story mean?
2. What do the people in the story discover about themselves or others by the end of the story?
3. What do the characters in the story discover about life by the end of the story?
4. What is the author's message to the reader?

▶ **Word Clues**

Read the sentences below. Look for the context clues that explain the underlined word.

The figure stood up, gradually stretching out its legs. It moved almost in slow motion, like an old man who had been <u>crouching</u> in one position too long.

If you do not know the meaning of the word *crouching* in the second sentence, read the first sentence. It explains the meaning of *crouching* by giving details about it. The details describe how the figure came out of a crouching position, by standing, and moving gradually, stretching out its legs. A crouching position is one of stooping low, with bent legs.

Use **detail** context clues to find the meaning of the three underlined words in the selection.

▶ **Strategy Tip**

As you read "Hopping Mad!" think about the message that the author is trying to tell the reader. What do you suppose the author wanted you to think by the end of the story? Use the questions about theme to help you figure out the story's theme.

HOPPING MAD!

Fwwwp! The welding torch went out. Nancy Fuentes rocked back onto her heels. She <u>eased</u> the tight-fitting welding mask off her head and wiped the sweat off her face with the back of her glove. The car was taking shape. But her welding was terrible. It was the only thing her dad hadn't taught her at the garage. Maybe the car wouldn't be finished in time for the contest!

There was a sudden, tiny grinding sound in back of her, and Nancy leaped to her feet. Her heart was pounding as she spun around.

"Fernando, don't you ever sneak up on me like that!" she shouted, almost dropping the welding torch.

Fernando grinned. The expression on his face was playful. "Sorry, Nan," he said. "I didn't want to <u>interrupt</u> your welding. And when you stopped, you just stood there. I shifted my weight, and my boot rolled over a pebble. That's what scared you." Fernando had on a clean white T-shirt and clean jeans. He worked in his uncle's garage a few blocks away, but he had obviously had time to clean up before coming to visit Nancy. Only the ground-in grime on his hands marked him as a fellow mechanic.

He looked at the car. It was a 1969 four-door that Nancy had bought a year ago. It was in really bad shape, but Nancy had been working hard to restore it. Now it was running fine, but the body needed a lot of work. In fact, it needed more work than usual because she was converting it into a "low rider."

A low rider is created when the springs are cut to lower the body about four inches. Low riders usually have special paint, body work, and inside decorations. Sometimes special lifting parts are put in so that the car can be

raised or lowered on its wheels. The lifters are sometimes powerful enough to make the car hop off the ground. There are low-rider clubs that have contests and award prizes to the best-looking or most unusual cars.

Nancy really wanted to win first prize in the Low-Rider Club's yearly contest. For one thing, she had already worked very hard. For another, no woman had ever won first prize. And finally, she could use the money. Her car had cost a lot to rebuild, and her savings were almost gone.

"You know, you've got some really tricky curves on those fenders. If I were you, I'd simplify the design." Fernando pointed to the welding that troubled Nancy. "Either that, or I could do the welding for you."

"No way," Nancy answered. She swallowed hard. She knew Fernando was one of the best welders in town. "I know you can do it. But then I'd never find out if I could do it. I'll try again tomorrow."

"The deadline is getting close," Fernando reminded her. "Do you even have a color picked out? Or a name?"

"I can't worry about colors or names now," Nancy replied. She walked away. "I have to close up the garage. Dad went home early to fix dinner."

Fernando started to say something more about the contest, but suddenly he had no one to talk to. Nancy had rolled the big door down between them. It didn't lock. The lock had been broken for years, but Fernando didn't try to open it. He just smiled and walked away.

The next morning, Nancy got to the garage just before her dad. She unlocked the pumps, got the cash drawer out of the safe, and opened the big door next to her car.

"Oh, no!" she yelled. "What happened?" Nancy started yelling and stomping around. She pounded the car with her fists. "No, no, no, no!" she yelled. Her father ran over to see what the problem was.

Nancy whirled around and stuck her face in front of his. "Did you do this?" she demanded.

"Do what?" said her father.

"This! This!" Nancy shouted, pointing to her car's fenders. The welding had been done, tricky curves and all.

Nancy saw that her father was looking confused. She backed off and patted him on the shoulder.

"Sorry, Dad," she said. "I just yelled at the first person I saw. Fernando did this. We were talking about it last night. When I get my hands on him . . ." Her voice started to rise again.

"Whoa, slow down," Mr. Fuentes said. "Look, you need a day away from this car, and I need parts from the city. Get the list from the office and take the pickup—some of the parts are heavy."

Nancy looked over her shoulder at the car. "It'll be here when you get back," her father said. "It's not going anywhere. And a day off will do you some good."

> *"Won't anyone let me finish this car by myself?"*

Reluctantly, Nancy got the list and drove off in the pickup.

The parts hadn't been ready when Nancy got to the city, and she had to wait for her order. When she got back to the garage, it was nearly dark. As she turned off the highway onto her street, she could see a bright light flickering in the garage. Someone was welding! Nancy gritted her teeth. Fernando was really going to get it now!

She parked the truck and ran toward the garage. A figure was bending over the left rear fender. She could see sparks flying. "Fernando, you get away from that car!" she shouted as loud as she could.

The figure stood up, gradually stretching out its legs. It moved almost in slow motion, like an old man who had been crouching in one position too long. In the middle of her yelling, Nancy noticed how familiar the motion was, and her voice trailed off into silence, as if someone was turning the volume down on a stereo. The figure was her dad.

"You, too?" Nancy said. "Won't anyone let me finish this car by myself?"

Mr. Fuentes put down the welding torch. "Have a look," he said.

Nancy brushed past him. There was the car, looking just as though Fernando had never touched it. "Wow!" she said, understanding at last. She turned and looked at him and then lowered her eyes a little. "Dad, how did you do that?" she asked quietly.

"I just undid everything Fernando did," her father replied. "I want this car to be all yours, too. Maybe I shouldn't have helped you either. But . . ."

Nancy threw her arms around him. "You did just the right thing," she said. "I got mad at you before I had all the facts. I should have known you wouldn't mess up my car."

Her father said, "You know, even Fernando was just trying to help. That doesn't excuse his barging in like that, I know."

"Yes, I shouldn't have pushed myself in like that." Fernando had walked into the garage and stood next to Nancy's father. "Your dad told me all about it—how angry you were and everything. I guess I wanted to show off what a great welder I was instead of just being a good friend. What I did wasn't any help at all. I came over to apologize."

"I accept. Anyway, you did help in one way," laughed Nancy.

"How's that?" Fernando asked.

"I'm going to get stronger lifters, paint the car bright red, and call it Hopping Mad."

RECALLING FACTS

1. Who are the characters in the story?

_____

_____

2. Who is Fernando? _____

_____

3. What kind of car is Nancy preparing?

_____

4. What is special about this kind of car?

_____

_____

5. What part of Nancy's work is she having trouble with? _____

_____

6. Where does Fernando work?

_____

_____

7. What does Fernando offer to do for Nancy?

_____

_____

8. Why does Nancy refuse the offer?

_____

_____

9. What does Fernando do that night?

_____

_____

10. How does Nancy feel about what Fernando did?

_____

_____

11. What does Nancy's father do while she is gone? _____

_____

12. Complete each sentence with the correct word from below.

     eased   interrupt   barging

  a. A rainstorm could _____ the World Series.

  b. The shoppers were _____ into the store for the huge sale.

  c. The child _____ the last puzzle piece into place.

INTERPRETING FACTS

1. Why do you think Nancy is so jumpy at the beginning of the story?

_____

_____

_____

_____

2. How does Fernando get into the garage to do the welding? _____

_____

3. What sort of person is Nancy?

_____

_____

_____

4. What sort of person is Fernando?

_____

_____

_____

5. What three reasons does Mr. Fuentes have for sending Nancy to the city? Which is the real reason? _____ _____

_____

_____

_____

6. How do you think Nancy feels after she sees what her father has done?

_____

_____

_____

_____

7. What do you think happens after the end of the story? Write a few sentences telling what happens.

_____

_____

_____

_____

The following questions will help you figure out the theme of "Hopping Mad!" Thinking about the title of the story and the people in the story will help you find the message behind the story.

1. *Title of the Story*

   What is the title of the story? ————————————————————————

   Who becomes extremely angry? ————————————————————————

   What two events brings on the anger?

   _____

   _____

   How does this person's anger cause trouble?

   _____

   _____

   Why is the title a good one for this story?

   _____

   _____

2. *People in the Story*

   What does Nancy learn about herself in the story?

   _____

   _____

   What does Fernando learn about himself in the story?

   _____

   _____

3. *Theme of the Story*

   What is the author's message to the reader?

   _____

   _____

   _____

   _____

▶ **Real Life Connections** Nancy was upset with her dad and Fernando because she wanted to finish the car herself. Have you ever felt like Nancy? Describe an experience.

Reading a Table

__Reading a Social Studies Selection _____

▶ Background Information

The history of automobiles is one of the most important and interesting stories in U.S. history. Did you know that in the 1890s cars were so new and so exciting that they were shown in circuses? Now cars are a symbol of the American way of life. America is a nation on wheels.

Cars made more than 20 years ago were very big and heavy, and they had large engines. These cars used a lot of gasoline. Large cars and higher speed limits meant that people had to buy and use a lot of gas. Both of these things contributed to the gas shortage in the 1970s.

Because of advances in technology, car makers are now able to build smaller cars that have been designed to use less gas. Using less gas saves people money. It also helps the environment by cutting down on the amount of pollution released into the air.

▶ Skill Focus

When reading textbooks, you will sometimes find **tables.** You should read tables very carefully. They will often give you information that is not found anywhere else in the selection.

Social studies and science selections often present information in the form of tables and charts. Presenting information in this way allows writers to give readers a lot of information in a small amount of space. Readers can learn a great deal of information from tables and charts, provided they know how to read them.

When reading a table, read the title first. Then use your finger to read down the columns and across the rows.

Turn to the first table on page 95. Read the title of the table. Then read down the left column. There you will find the number of miles per gallon that a car might get. Read across the top to find out how much a gallon of gas might cost. Then read across each row to find out how much a person would pay for gas in one year.

Follow the same three steps to read the table on page 96, reading the title first, then the left column, across the top, and finally across each row.

▶ Word Clues

Read the sentences below. Look for the context clues that explain the underlined word.

This table shows how much a <u>consumer</u> would pay for gas each year to go 12,000 miles. A consumer is a person who buys and uses goods.

If you do not know the word *consumer* in the first sentence, read on to the next sentence. The words *a person who buys and uses goods* tell the meaning of *consumer*. A word meaning that is stated directly can often be found before or after a new word.

Use **definition** context clues to find the meaning of the three underlined words in the selection.

▶ Strategy Tip

As you read, "Gassing Up–or Down?" study the tables carefully. The first table tells how much it costs to buy gas for a car during one year. The second table tells how much gas people use in various countries and how many people usually ride in a car. These tables give readers information that is not found in the selection.

Gassing Up–or Down?

How often does a car need gas? If you have a family car, how often do you visit a gas station? once a week? once a month? every few days? How far does your car go between fill-ups? How far does your car go for each gallon it burns? What does it cost to buy gas for one year?

The table below shows how much a consumer would pay for gas each year to go 12,000 miles. A consumer is a person who buys and uses goods.

Cost of Gasoline at 12,000 Miles per Year					
	Cost per gallon				
	$1.00	1.25	1.50	1.75	2.00
10	$1200.00	1500.00	1800.00	2100.00	2400.00
15	800.00	1000.00	1200.00	1400.00	1600.00
Miles per Gallon 20	600.00	750.00	900.00	1050.00	1200.00
25	480.00	600.00	720.00	840.00	960.00
30	400.00	500.00	600.00	700.00	800.00
35	343.00	429.00	514.00	600.00	686.00
40	300.00	375.00	450.00	525.00	600.00

Buying the Cheap Stuff

Gas used to be very cheap in the United States. Companies bought oil cheaply from overseas and turned it into gasoline. The government encouraged the low prices and did not tax gas much. Americans became used to larger and larger cars that took a lot of gas to run. The amount of gas a car uses depends on the car's size and weight, along with the design of the engine.

Gas in Western Europe and Japan, however, was a different story. Gas was very expensive in these places, partly because governments put high taxes on gas to raise money. Cars built in Western Europe and Japan were generally small and light, and they used much less gasoline.

Then, in 1973, some of the countries that sold oil to the United States stopped selling it. There was a huge gas shortage. The price of oil products, including gasoline, rose sharply. Gas became scarce, and there were long lines at gas stations. There was also gas rationing, in which people could get gas only every other day. The prices stayed high when the oil-producing countries started to sell oil again in 1974. Suddenly, it had become very expensive to run a car. Some changes were needed so that Americans would never experience a gas shortage again.

People started buying smaller cars, mostly those made in Japan. American car makers hurried to design smaller, more <u>efficient</u> cars because the Japanese had cars that didn't waste gas. However, they had been surprised by the sudden rise in gas prices. The American companies had financial problems while they were trying to catch up with Japan. They did not know how to make small cars, and they couldn't make them as cheaply as the Japanese.

American car makers eventually figured things out. They made smaller cars. They became partners with some of the Japanese companies. Look in any parking lot today. You will see mostly smaller cars. Many of them have Japanese names, such as Nissan, Toyota, Honda, or Mitsubishi. But names can fool you. These cars are not all <u>imports.</u> Imports are goods made in a foreign country. Some cars with Japanese names are now made in the United States. And some cars with American names are now built in Japan. The important fact about these cars, however, is that they use much less gas than their gas-guzzling cousins of the 1970s.

Why is it important to use less gas? Here are three reasons. First, people do not want to spend any more money than they have to. As long as gas prices are high, it makes sense to buy less of it. Second, the world's oil supply is not unlimited. The world will someday run out of oil. Since gasoline is one of the most common uses of oil, it make sense not to use it up quickly. Third, burning gas causes pollution. The exhaust of a car has a lot of poison in it. The atmosphere can take only so much. Even the nonpoisonous gas, carbon dioxide, is bad for the atmosphere.

> *If you live near a street that people use for getting to work, notice how many people are in each car.*

Less Is More

Because smaller cars burn less gasoline, we are using less. Cars may become even more efficient in the future. But we may still need to change some habits so that we use even less gas. How can we use less gasoline? We could drive less. That is sometimes difficult. Our cities are farther apart than those in Europe or Japan. Many of our cities are very large. People often live far from where they work. And bus or train transportation is often inconvenient and expensive.

We could still manage to drive less, however. Many people take a car to go very short distances, such as under a mile. They lose out on getting good exercise, and they are hard on their cars and the environment. Short-distance driving can wear out a car quickly. Also, short trips cause more pollution. That is because the engine never gets hot enough to use gas efficiently.

✔ If you live near a street that people use for getting to work, notice how many people are in each car. You're likely to see just one, the driver, or perhaps the driver and one passenger. In fact, the average number of people in a car is just 1.8 in the United States. As you can see in the table, the average number of people in a car in other countries is higher—as high as 4 in Japan. A car's gallons-per-person figure is even better if you add people to the car.

Gasoline Use and Number of Persons per Car		
	Gallons used per person each year	**Persons per car**
Italy	87	2.4
Netherlands	83	2.8
France	127	2.5
Germany (western)	159	2.1
Belgium	99	3.8
United Kingdom	152	2.9
Japan	94	4.0
United States	432	1.8

The table also shows how many gallons each person uses each year. Clearly, we could do better in not using our cars so much, and in sharing rides.

What to Do?

Using less gasoline may be a good idea, but how can we get people to do it? You can talk to your parents, of course, and ask them to walk more. You can offer to walk on errands, or take your bike. You can talk to people about sharing rides.

Government leaders can help, too. They can <u>legislate</u>; that is, they can pass laws that will make it cheaper and more convenient to take buses and trains. They can make gas more expensive by raising the taxes on it. The United States has a very low tax rate on gas. In 1993, the tax rate was 33 cents a gallon. In Italy, it was $2.37—over seven times as much as the U.S. tax rate. Raising taxes could make the car less attractive. People might be more careful about using their cars. On the other hand, people who must drive a lot, such as

salespeople, taxi drivers, and delivery people, would have a difficult time. How would you balance things? Would you raise taxes a lot right away? Would you raise taxes just a little? Would you leave things the way they are?

RECALLING FACTS

1. Match each of the following causes with its effect.

Cause

_____ The people who sold gas to the United States stopped selling it.

_____ People in the United States drive almost everywhere, both for long trips and for short trips.

_____ Gas remained expensive after the gas shortage of 1973.

_____ Gas was very cheap in the United States.

_____ American car makers were not prepared for the gas shortage.

Effect

a. More gas is used in the United States than anywhere else.

b. People bought smaller cars that were mostly foreign imports. American car makers began to design smaller cars.

c. Car makers had financial problems because Americans were not buying as many cars.

d. People got used to buying larger and larger cars.

e. Gasoline became scarce, and prices went up sharply.

2. What kind of car can go farther on a gallon of gas? _____

_____

3. What are some advantages to using less gasoline? _____

_____

4. What are two ways to use less gasoline?

_____

_____

5. What would happen if the government raised gas taxes? _____

_____

6. Read the paragraph with the check mark next to it. Underline the sentence that tells the main idea of the paragraph.

7. Complete each sentence with the correct word from below.

efficient   imports   legislate

a. A kind of tractor made in Japan is used on many farms in the United States. These tractors are

_____.

b. Evan is able to do all his homework, clean his room, and walk the dog before dinnertime. He is very

_____.

c. Congress can pass laws. Its members have the power to _____.

INTERPRETING FACTS

1. Write F or O next to each sentence to tell whether it is a fact or an opinion.

____ a. Smaller cars generally use less gasoline than larger cars.

____ b. Gas prices were very low before the gas shortage of 1973.

____ c. People should be free to drive anywhere and any time they want.

____ d. Smaller cars are better in every way than larger cars.

____ e. In the United States, there are fewer riders per car than in other countries.

____ f. Higher gas taxes will ruin the country.

2. Find two facts in the selection that support the following opinion.

It is important for people in the United States to use less gasoline.

a. _____

_____

_____

b. _____

_____

_____

3. Which of the following sentences best tells the main idea of the selection? Circle its letter.

a. The countries that sell oil to the United States could stop again at any time.

b. Because the price of gasoline has gone up sharply, people are driving smaller, lighter cars and are thinking about ways of using less gasoline.

c. Smaller cars have become so popular in the past twenty years that American car makers have joined with Japanese car makers to make smaller cars.

Turn to the table on page 95. To understand this table, read down the left column first. There you will find the number of miles per gallon a car might get. Then read across the top of the table to see how much a gallon of gas might cost. Now read across each row to see how much you would have to spend in a year if you drove 12,000 miles.

1. What is the title of the table? _____

2. What is the best miles-per-gallon number? _____

3. What is the lowest cost per gallon in the table? _____

4. What is the highest cost per year? What are the miles per gallon and cost per gallon for the highest cost? _____

5. If gasoline costs $1.75 a gallon, how much would you spend for a car that gets 30 miles per gallon? _____

6. Imagine that gasoline costs $1.50 a gallon. You can afford no more than $600.00 a year for gas. What kind of gas mileage must your car get? _____

Turn to the table on page 96. To understand this table, read down the left column first. There you will find the names of several countries. Then read the labels at the top. These lables tell the number of gallons of gasoline used by each person every year and the number of persons in each car. Read across the rows to find the numbers.

1. In which country are the most gallons used per person? _____

2. In which countries are three or more people in the car for a typical car ride?

_____

3. In which country are fewer than two people in the car for a typical car ride?

_____

4. Which country uses the least amount of gasoline per person each year?

_____

5. Which countries use more than 100 gallons of gasoline per person each year?

_____

6. Which country is the closest to the United States in the number of people per car?

_____

▶ **Real Life Connections** What advice would you give to the mayor of your city or selectmen in your community to get people to use less gasoline?

Diagrams

___ Reading a Science Selection

▶ Background Information

Throughout your life, you will have to read things that contain **diagrams**, or pictures. For example, instructions often have diagrams to help people understand what they are supposed to do. You are probably already familiar with the diagrams in instructions.

Science articles also often have diagrams to help readers understand a topic better. For example, understanding how an automobile engine works can seem very complicated. It will seem much simpler, however, if you understand the different parts and how they work together. The selection that follows explains how a car engine works.

▶ Skill Focus

When reading a selection with diagrams, remember to study each diagram as you read the text. If a diagram has a **caption**, read that first. The caption is like a title. It tells what the diagram is about.

In many diagrams, you will also find **labels**. Labels name the parts of the objects shown in the diagram. Sometimes a paragraph describes something that you have never seen. When you see a picture of the object labeled in a diagram, you will understand it better. Sometimes you will need to study a diagram and read the paragraph that goes with it several times. In this way, you can work with the words and diagrams together to understand the ideas in the selection.

When you are reading a selection that has diagrams, use the following steps.

1. Read the paragraph before each diagram. Then study the diagram and read the caption that goes with it. If there are labels, read them while studying the diagram. The paragraph below the diagram may explain what is pictured. Read that paragraph, too.
2. Slowly read the rest of the paragraphs. Look back at the diagrams whenever you think they will help.
3. After you have finished reading the paragraphs and studying the diagrams, look away from the reading. Try to picture what you have read and the details in the diagrams. If you are not able to do this, read the paragraphs and study the diagrams again.

4. Work in this way until you understand all the ideas in the selection.

▶ Word Clues

Diagrams can be used as a kind of context clue. If you are unfamiliar with the term *intake stroke*, you would read the text and look at the diagram on page 101. The diagram shows part of an automobile engine. It shows the four steps in the operation of a cylinder. Step 1 of the diagram shows you that the *intake stroke* occurs when the piston moves down, allowing air and gasoline to move into the cylinder.

Use **diagram** context clues to find the meanings of the four underlined terms in the selection.

▶ Strategy Tip

Science selctions often contain diagrams. Diagrams help readers visualize, or see, what the author is writing about. While you read, study the diagrams carefully. You may want to go back and forth from the words in the selection to the diagrams several times.

WHAT MAKES A CAR RUN?

The heart of the automobile is the engine. The first successful American gasoline engine was invented in 1892 by Frank and Henry Duryea. The gas engine became successful very quickly. Blacksmith shops that made horseshoes were soon changed into service stations and garages. The gasoline engine has become more complicated since the early days of the automobile, but the idea is still the same. Gasoline has to be mixed with air and burned. The gasoline and air mixture burns at a high temperature. The following paragraphs explain how and where the mixture burns.

How the Gasoline Engine Works

All the parts of a car engine work together. An important part of the engine is a hollow metal tube called a **cylinder** (SIL ən dər). Tightly fitted inside the cylinder is a solid piece of steel called a **piston** (PIS tən). It is here, in the cylinders, that air and gasoline are mixed and the gasoline is burned. The gasoline burns so fast and at such a high temperature that it produces hot gases. When the gasoline burns, the cylinder is tightly closed. The gases are under great pressure. This rapid burning is called an **explosion** (ik SPLOH zhən). The spark that causes the explosion is made by a spark plug. An automobile engine gets its power from hundreds of small but powerful explosions. The earliest gasoline engines had only one cylinder. Today's gasoline engines have four, six, or eight cylinders.

How the Cylinders Work

✔ Look at the diagrams in Figure 1. Each diagram shows one of the four steps in the operation of a cylinder. Each step is called a stroke. The piston moves down during the intake stroke. At the same time, the air and gasoline mixture moves into the cylinder (step one). As the piston moves upward, the mixture is compressed, or squeezed into a smaller space. This is the compression stroke (step two). Next comes the power stroke. A spark is given off by the spark plug. The air and gasoline mixture explodes. The pressure of the explosion forces the piston down (step three). This is followed by an exhaust stroke, when the gases produced by the explosion are forced out of the cylinder (step four). As the pistons move up and down, they move the piston rods. Look at Figure 1 again.

How the Power is Sent to the Wheels

The up-and-down motion of the pistons produces power. But to move a car forward, the up-and-down motion has to be changed to a turning or spinning motion. Piston rods connect the pistons to the backbone of the engine, the **crankshaft** (KRANK shaft). As the pistons move up and down, they move the piston rods. The piston rods then turn the crankshaft. The crankshaft changes the up-and-down motion to a spinning motion. As the crankshaft turns, it spins the flywheel. In most cars, the spinning power is carried to the rear wheels that move the car. Look at Figure 2.

Figure 1. These diagrams show the four strokes in the operation of a cylinder.

1. **Intake Stroke** 2. **Compression Stroke** 3. **Power Stroke** 4. **Exhaust Stroke**

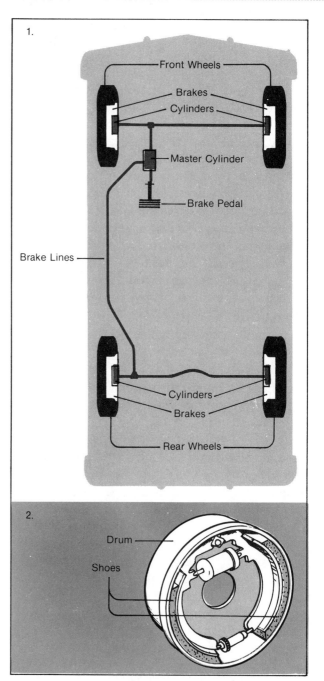

Figure 2. Part 1 shows how the pistons turn the crankshaft and the crankshaft turns the flywheel. Part 2 shows how power is carried to the wheels.

Figure 3. The engine is cooled by water. The water is cooled by air that is blown by the fan.

Figure 4. Part 1 shows the whole hydraulic brake system. Part 2 shows a drum brake inside a wheel.

How the Engine is Cooled

When gasoline burns inside the cylinders, the temperature can get as high as 4,500° Fahrenheit, or 2,481° Celsius. This much heat can melt iron and speed up rusting. Because of the heat that can build up, a gasoline engine must have a cooling system. The job of the cooling system is to remove heat from the metal parts. Water stored in the **radiator** (RAY dee ayt ər) does the job. A pump moves the water through the engine and cools the cylinders. In doing this, the water also gets very hot. It has to be cooled. This is the job of the fan. Look at Figure 3. In very cold weather, antifreeze is added to the water. The antifreeze helps keep the water from freezing.

How the Brakes Work

The braking system is used to slow or stop a car. **Hydraulic** (hy DRAW lik) brakes are used in today's cars. Hydraulic brakes use liquid pressure. When the driver presses the brake pedal, liquid is forced from the master cylinder through the brake lines, or tubes, to the wheel cylinders. (Neither the master cylinder nor the wheel cylinders have anything to do with the engine cylinders.) The liquid forces the brake shoes against the brake drums inside the wheels. The drums rub against the wheels and stop them from turning. Disk brakes work differently from drum brakes, but they are also operated by hydraulic pressure. Look at Figure 4.

RECALLING FACTS

1. Write the following steps in the order in which they occur in a cylinder: compression stroke, intake stroke, exhaust stroke, power stroke.

   a. _____

   b. _____

   c. _____

   d. _____

2. Who invented the first successful American automobile engine?

   _____

   _____

3. In what part of the engine is the gasoline burned?

   _____

   _____

4. What provides the spark that causes the gasoline to explode?

   _____

   _____

5. What moves up and down, causing the piston rods to move?

   _____

   _____

6. What cools the water in the engine?

   _____

   _____

7. Where are the brake drums?

   _____

   _____

8. Reread the selection paragraph that has a check mark next to it. Underline the sentence that has the main idea.

9. Use Figures 1 and 2 on pages 101 and 102 to answer the following questions.

   a. Does the piston move up or down during the compression stroke?

   _____

   _____

   b. Does the piston move up or down during the power stroke?

   _____

   _____

   c. Where do the burning gases go out during the exhaust stroke?

   _____

   _____

   d. What causes the flywheel to spin?

   _____

   _____

For questions 1-3, place a check mark in the box next to the word that completes each sentence.

1. An engine with eight cylinders would probably be _____ powerful than an engine with four cylinders.
   ☐ **a.** less ☐ **b.** equally ☐ **c.** more

2. When a car is moving along a highway, the pistons move up and down
   ☐ **a.** very quickly.
   ☐ **b.** and from side to side.
   ☐ **c.** very slowly.

3. In cars with front-wheel drive, the power is carried to the _____ wheels.
   ☐ **a.** rear ☐ **b.** front ☐ **c.** side

4. What causes the water in an engine's cooling system to get hot?

   _____

   _____

   _____

5. Why is the engine referred to as the heart of the automobile?

   _____

   _____

   _____

   _____

SKILL FOCUS

Write the answers to the following questions on the lines provided.

1. In Figure 1, what causes the power stroke? _____

   _____

2. In Figure 2, what turns the flywheel? _____

3. In Figure 3, what moves the water through the engine? _____

4. In Figure 4, what does the brake fluid move through to get from the master cylinder to the brake cylinder? _____

5. Explain in your own words the four-stroke operation of a cylinder as shown in Figure 1.

   _____

   _____

   _____

   _____

▶ **Real Life Connections** In the future, do you think cars will be powered by electricity or some source other than gasoline? Give reasons for your response.

Large Numbers

Reading a Mathematics Selection

▶ Background Information

Numbers are a very important part of life. The number of friends coming to your house, the amount of money you have in your pocket or purse, or the number of students in a classroom are all described by our number system.

However, the system that we use today is certainly not the first numerical system ever used. After all, there have been many great civilizations, including the Egyptian, Greek, Roman, and Arab civilizations. Early peoples like us, needed numerical systems to help them in their everyday lives.

Believe it or not, as early as 3000 B.C.E., the Egyptians were using a numerical system. This system used hieroglyphics, or picture writing. They based this system on the number 10, just like we do today. This system, however, was difficult to write. There had to be a picture for every number. Because of this, it was difficult to read and write large numbers.

Another interesting fact is that the Egyptian numerical system did not include a symbol for zero. The first system that used a symbol for zero was the Hindu-Arabic numerical system. This system was developed in 500 B.C.E. Of all the ancient systems, the Hindu-Arabic system was the most complete. For this reason, we adopted this system, and it is still used all around the world.

As you read above, even early peoples struggled with reading large numbers. Large numbers can sometimes be intimidating. When you look at a number like 1,334,768,765, you may be overwhelmed. This feeling is natural. But you can overcome this feeling by understanding a few of the key terms needed to read large numbers.

In "Place Value," you will learn new words that are important to understanding some concepts in mathematics and in learning how to read large numbers. As you read the selection, pay attention to the function of zero in large numbers.

▶ Skill Focus

The value of a **digit**, or numeral, in a number depends on the position, or place, of the digit. This position is called **place value.**

For example, the digit 9 in the number 93 has a value different from the digit 9 in the number 39.

▶ Word Clues

When you finish reading the selection, you should understand the meanings of the words *digit, place value,* and *place holder.* The selection has several examples that will help you with the meanings of these words.

▶ Strategy Tip

Knowing the place value of each digit in a numeral will help you to understand large numbers. Learning how commas are used in large numbers will help you read them.

Place Value

When a number has four, five, or six digits, a comma is usually used to separate the three digits, or numbers, at the right from the others. The digits to the left of the comma are read as *thousands*. You first read the digits to the left of the comma. Then add the word *thousands*.

For example, beginning at the left and reading toward the right, the number 487,216 is read as four hundred eighty-seven thousand, two hundred sixteen.

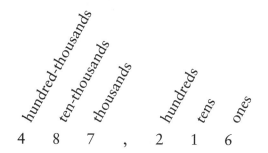

The place value of each digit is shown above each number.

The 4 means 4 hundred-thousands,
or ──────────────────────→400,000
The 8 means 8 ten-thousands, or ──→ 80,000
The 7 means 7 thousands, or ──────→ 7,000
The 2 means 2 hundreds, or ───────→ 200
The 1 means 1 ten, or ──────────→ 10
The 6 means 6 ones, or ─────────→ 6
                              ─────────
                                487,216

The number 325,007 is read as three hundred twenty-five thousand, seven.

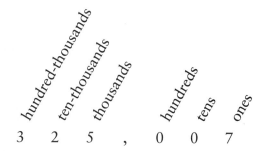

When reading large numbers that have one comma, the comma should signal you to say the word *thousand*.

Also, do not use the word *and* to connect parts of the number. For example:

5,611   five thousand, six hundred eleven

The word *and* is used only when reading dollars and cents. The *and* is used between the dollars and cents.

$8,684.54   eight thousand, six hundred eighty-four dollars *and* fifty-four cents

✔ Zero is used as a place holder. In the number 589,068, the zero holds the place for hundreds. It tells you that there are no hundreds in the number. The number is read as five hundred eighty-nine thousand, sixty-eight.

RECALLING FACTS

1. When there are more than three digits in a number, a comma is used to separate the _____ digits at the right from the other digits.

2. The value of the place to the left of hundreds is _____.

3. The value of the place to the left of ten-thousands is _____.

4. _____ is used as a place holder.

5. Reread the paragraph with a check mark next to it. Draw a line under the sentence that states the main idea.

6. Write the meaning for each of the
   following words.

digit: _____

place value: _____ _____

place holder: _____

Circle the letter of the word that completes each sentence.

1. The value of the digit in the place that is
   on the far _____ affects the total
   value of a number most.

   a. left   **b.** right

2. In the number 4,932, raising the value of
   the digit 9 would cause the place to the
   left of it to _____.

   a. increase   **b.** decrease

3. Zero _____ affect the value of a
   number if it is in the first place on the far
   left of the number.

   a. does   **b.** does not

4. In the number 9,710, decreasing the value
   of the digit 1 would cause the place value
   to the right of it to _____.

   a. increase   **b.** decrease

SKILL FOCUS

A. Read the number words below. Then rewrite them using numbers. Remember to put in
commas and zeros where they are needed.

1. Six thousand, two hundred fifteen _____

2. Ten thousand, seven hundred eighty-eight _____

3. Nine thousand, four _____

4. Seven hundred sixty-four thousand, two hundred ninety _____

5. Four hundred forty thousand, two hundred six _____

6. Three hundred thousand, five hundred twenty _____

7. Nine hundred forty thousand, five hundred two _____

8. Eighty-six thousand, fifty _____

9. Five hundred twenty-eight thousand, four hundred seventy-nine _____

10. Sixty-three thousand, four hundred seventeen _____

B. Rewrite each of the following numbers in words. Include commas where they are needed.

1. 2,008 _____

_____

2. $348.22 _____

_____

3. 240,000 _____

_____

4. 4,682 _____

_____

5. 75,343 _____

_____

6. 279,600 _____

_____

7. $3,001.18 _____

_____

8. $243,078 _____

_____

9. $89,266.16 _____

_____

C. Rewrite each group of three number words as numbers on the lines at the right. Add up the three numbers and write the sum as a number and then, at the left, as number words.

1. one hundred twenty-seven thousand, four hundred twenty   _____

   sixty thousand, four hundred twenty-eight   _____

   thirty-two   + _____

   _____   _____

2. six hundred thirty-six thousand, forty   _____

   three   _____

   five hundred fifteen   + _____

   _____   _____

▶ **Real Life Connections** For what type of job would you need to be able to read large numbers?

Lesson 37

Accented Syllable and Schwa

When words contain two syllables, one of the syllables is stressed, or accented, more than the other. In dictionaries, the **accent mark** (') is placed at the end of the syllable that is said with more stress. For example, the first syllable in *funny* is said with more stress than the second syllable.

fun' ny

Say each of the following words to yourself. Write an accent mark after the syllable that is accented.

mar' ket	sur prise	plas tic	be fore	pic nic
or chard	bas ket	won der	no tice	al low
ho tel	de pend	proc ess	rad ish	friend ly
farm er	poul try	or der	pro tect	a mount
drag on	prod uct	spark ling	chick en	

Sometimes the vowels *a, e, i, o,* and *u* all have the same sound. This is a soft sound like a short *u* pronounced very lightly.

Pronounce *balloon.* Did the *a* sound like a soft, short *u*?

Pronounce *children.* Did the *e* sound like a soft, short *u*?

Pronounce *easily.* Did the *i* sound like a soft, short *u*?

Pronounce *confuse.* Did the *o* sound like a soft, short *u*?

Pronounce *support.* Did the *u* sound like a soft, short *u*?

When any one of the five vowels has this sound, it is called the **schwa** sound.

Place an accent mark where it belongs in each of the words below. Then underline the letter that stands for the schwa sound in each word. The first word is marked for you.

<u>a</u> bout'	o pen	jew el	a loud	wool en
cab in	cen tral	suc cess	sof ten	par ent
pi lot	A pril	meth od	kitch en	so da
wal rus	sup pose	post er	po lice	cir cus
prob lem	pur pose	sev en	wag on	

Look back at the words in the list above. Does the **schwa** sound come in the accented syllable or the unaccented syllable? Write the correct word in the sentence below.

The schwa sound always falls in an ———————————— syllable of a word.

In most dictionaries, the schwa sound is shown by the symbol ə. When you see this symbol in a dictionary respelling, you now know that it stands for the schwa sound and that it is pronounced like a soft, short *u*.

Syllables

You have learned guides for dividing two-syllable compound words and words with double consonants into syllables. A third guide shows you how to divide into syllables words that have a prefix or a suffix.

Words with a Prefix or Suffix

A **prefix** is a word part that is added to the beginning of a root word to change its meaning. The prefixes *re* and *un* have one vowel sound. When added to a word, they form their own syllable.

unwrap   un wrap

A **suffix** is a word part that is added to the end of a root word. The suffixes *er* and *ness* have one vowel sound. When added to a word, they form their own syllable.

painter   paint er

When a two-syllable word has a prefix or suffix, you divide it into syllables between the prefix or suffix and the root word.

Divide each word below into two syllables by writing each syllable separately on the line to the right of the word.

Dividing Words with Prefixes

1. unsafe _____   3. preview _____   7. exchange _____

2. refill _____   5. dislike _____   8. untrue _____

3. subway _____   6. refund _____   9. disband _____

Dividing Words with Suffixes

1. farmer _____   3. useful _____   5. careful _____

2. rarely _____   4. fewer _____   6. treeless _____

Fill in the words necessary to complete the following guide.

Guide 3: A word that has a prefix or _____ is divided into syllables between the prefix or suffix and the _____ word.

Dividing Compound Words

1. sidewalk _____   4. wishbone _____   7. snapshot _____

2. barefoot _____   5. football _____   8. sundown _____

3. rainfall _____   6. textbook _____   9. spaceship _____

Dividing Words with Double Consonants

1. trapper _____   3. cabbage _____   5. ladder _____

2. correct _____   4. button _____   6. barren _____

Fact and Opinion

How many advertisements do you hear or read each day? You hear them on radio and television, and you read them in magazines and newspapers.

Most advertisements contain both **fact and opinion.** The writer of the ad hopes that the reader or listener will believe the whole ad. A good reader is able to sort out facts and opinions and decide how much to believe. How do you tell the difference? Look at these two statements:

a. Flakies are good for you.

b. A cup of Flakies gives you 60 grams of protein, all the protein needed in a day.

Which sentence states a fact and which states an opinion? A fact can always be checked. You can find out if it's true or not. Therefore, *b* is a statement of fact. You still don't know if it's true, but at least it can be checked. Statement *a* is an opinion. What does "good for you" mean? Perhaps you agree with the opinion, but you cannot check it. When you see words, such as *good, better, terrible, pretty,* or *ugly,* you are reading someone's opinion. There is nothing wrong with opinions, but a careful listener or reader should be able to tell the difference between opinion and fact.

The following statements might be found in an ad. Some contain facts and some contain opinions. If the statement contains a fact, fill in the circle before the word **fact.** If the statement contains an opinion, fill in the circle before the word **opinion.**

1. Everyone thinks that the Zippy is the car of the future.

   ○ fact   ○ opinion

2. Road tests show that the Zippy gets 45 miles per gallon in highway driving.

   ○ fact   ○ opinion

3. Zippy carries a warranty on 50,000 miles or 12 months, whichever comes first.

   ○ fact   ○ opinion

4. Famous race car driver, Hotrod Harry, says, "Buy a Zippy! It's the best car on the road."

   ○ fact   ○ opinion

5. The Zippy has an air-cooled engine.

   ○ fact   ○ opinion

6. All the Zippy dealers are good people.

   ○ fact   ○ opinion

7. We offer more attractive rates for longer leases.

   ○ fact   ○ opinion

8. All Zippy cars come with air conditioning.

   ○ fact   ○ opinion

9. Zippy dealers go wild on convertible prices.

   ○ fact   ○ opinion

10. Pound for pound, dollar for dollar, Zippy is the best car in the world.

    ○ fact   ○ opinion

11. Now through April 1, all new Zippy cars have a $300 rebate.

    ○ fact   ○ opinion

12. Zippy model T14 comes with a CD player at no extra charge.

    ○ fact   ○ opinion

Main Idea and Supporting Details

Many times in reading, you will look for the **main idea and supporting details**. Details give more information about the main idea. They are called supporting details because they support the main idea.

Below is a paragraph about how the brakes work in a car. After the paragraph, its main idea and the supporting details are listed.

Braking a car is an interesting process. In most cars, a liquid called brake fluid begins the steps that stop the moving automobile. When the brakes are not being used, the fluid rests in the master cylinder and the brake tubes. When the driver steps on the brake pedal, the fluid is pushed toward the brake shoe. The brake shoe presses against the brake drum, stopping the wheel. Each wheel has its own braking system.

Main Idea   Braking a car is an interesting process.

Supporting Details

a. In most cars, a liquid called brake fluid begins the steps that stop the moving automobile.

b. When the brakes are not being used, the fluid rests in the master cylinder and the brake tubes.

c. When the driver steps on the brake pedal, the fluid is pushed toward the brake shoe.

d. The brake shoe presses against the brake drum, stopping the wheel.

e. Each wheel has its own braking system.

On the next page, write the main idea and three supporting details for each paragraph.

1. In the United States, almost everyone's life is linked to the auto industry. Most people depend on a car, bus, or truck for transportation. More than 12 million people earn their living in some part of the car industry by building, shipping, servicing, or selling cars, buses, or trucks. These people account for about one tenth of the labor force. In fact, there are 500,000 automobile-related businesses in the United States.

2. Several steps go into designing a new car model. Automobile designers create hundreds of sketches on computers. Final ideas for the new model come from these sketches. Then a full-sized clay model is made. Further improvements are made in the design. A fiberglass model is made. Finally, when every part has been approved, blueprints of the car are drawn so that the car can be cut out of steel and built.

3. Most of the early automobile builders were mechanics or knew about machines before they built cars. Ransom E. Olds made gasoline engines for farm equipment. Henry Ford was an engineer in a power house. Alexander Winton repaired bicycles. Elwood Haynes was in charge of a gas company.

4. When cars were first made, most drivers did not go past the city limits in case the "horseless buggy" broke down. Drivers had to wear goggles because there were no windshields to keep dust and dirt from their eyes. Women had to tie their hats on their heads with scarves to keep the hats from blowing off. Everyone wore linen dusters to protect clothes against the clouds of dust from the dirt roads. The early days of cars were an adventure.

5. Today the manufacture of cars is aided by technology. Computer-aided manufacturing (CAM) directs computers to make car parts. It also directs robots in performing assembly tasks. To insure quality in all stages of the assembly, cars are inspected by lasers.

Paragraph 1

Main Idea _____

Supporting Details

   a. _____

   b. _____

     _____

   c. _____

Paragraph 2

Main Idea _____

Supporting Details

   a. _____

   b. _____

   c. _____

     _____

Paragraph 3

Main Idea _____

Supporting Details

   a. _____

   b. _____

   c. _____

Paragraph 4

Main Idea _____

Supporting Details

   a. _____

   b. _____

   c. _____

Paragraph 5

Main Idea _____

Supporting Details

   a. _____

   b. _____

   c. _____

Table of Contents

Sometimes you may need to find information about a certain subject in several books. To locate the information that you need, you should use the **table of contents** in each book.

The table of contents is found at the beginning of a book. A table of contents lists the titles of the chapters and gives the page on which each chapter begins. Sometimes a table of contents gives the most important topics included in each chapter. It may also give the page on which each topic begins.

To use a table of contents, glance through the title and topics until you find one that has to do with your subject. Then turn to the page number given next to the chapter title or topic and read until you find the information. In this way, you don't have to "leaf through" the whole book. You can locate the information that you want quickly.

Below is a table of contents from a book about automobiles. To answer the questions that follow it, use two steps.

1. Look at the chapter titles to find out in which chapter you might find the information asked for.

2. Read through the topics under that title to find out on which page the topic in the question begins.

Contents

1. Suppose you wish to find information about the auto industry at the present time.

   a. Under which chapter title would you look? _____

   b. On which page would you start to read? _____

2. Suppose you wish to find information about the drive train in a car.

   a. Under which chapter title would you look? _____

   b. On which page would you start to read? _____

3. Suppose you wish to find information about different kinds of early cars.

   a. Under which chapter title would you look? _____

   b. On which page would you start to read? _____

4. Suppose you wish to find out the kinds of materials used in building a car.

   a. Under which chapter title would you look? _____

   b. On which page would you start to read? _____

5. Suppose you wish to find information about the problems of pollution and auto safety.

   a. Under which chapter title would you look? _____

   b. On which page would you start to read? _____

6. Suppose you wish to find information about a career as an auto salesperson.

   a. Under which chapter title would you look? _____

   b. On which page would you start to read? _____

7. Suppose you wish to find information about Henry Ford.

   a. Under which chapter title would you look? _____

   b. On which page would you start to read? _____

8. Suppose you wish to find information about research and testing of cars.

   a. Under which chapter title would you look? _____

   b. On which page would you start to read? _____

9. Suppose you wish to find information about car production in Japan.

   a. Under which chapter title would you look? _____

   b. On which page would you start to read? _____

10. Suppose you wish to find information about the brake system.

    a. Under which chapter title would you look? _____

    b. On which page would you start to read? _____

Lesson 42

Comparing Car Ads

If you are interested in buying a new car, reading ads in newspapers and magazines should start you in the right direction. The details in ads can help you decide what kind of car will suit your needs and your budget. After you decide on the best car for your needs, you shop around for the best price.

Carefully read the following ads to compare the two cars.

PASHUBI: WE DESIGNED OUR CAR FOR ■ *YOU* ■ *THE* DRIVER

At Pashubi, we think you are very important. So we created the 630-X, a fully equipped luxury sports car. The 630-X surrounds the driver with more window than other sports cars. The 630-X has a steering wheel and instrument panel that can be moved up or down.

The roomy bucket seats can be easily moved and can tilt back as far as you like. And the large storage area in back lifts up to become two additional seats.

There are 30 standard equipment features, including power disc brakes, power windows, electrically heated outside rearview mirror, two-tone paint, and CD player.

At $20,025, the 630-X offers more than other imported cars. And you'll save on gas—an exceptional 43 EST HWY MPG, 28 EST MPG. Use MPG for comparison. Mileage may differ depending on conditions. Highway mileage may be less.

The 630-X. By Pashubi. It's *not* for everyone—but it is for *you*.

TILTON:
The American way to get more for your money.

You get more for your money with our cars. Take the Star, for example. This compact car uses 3,000 computer-assisted robot welds, more than any other car. This helps to create an easy-to-maintain car which will give you more for your money for years to come.

The Star gives you more for your money because it's sensibly priced. It starts as low as

$16,999*. The Star gives you more for your money with front-wheel drive. With the engine pulling in front and rack-and-pinion steering, you get the real feel of the road.

The six-passenger Star gives you more for your money with comfort.

And the Star gives you more for your money when you study the mileage figures:

41 EST HWY, 26 EST MPG.+

The Star's standard equipment includes power disc brakes, CD player, and 5-speed transmission (3-speed automatic is extra). Among the other extras are two-tone paint, luggage rack, leather steering wheel, power windows, and more.

Last year's Star was the best-selling compact car. See the Star today—and learn how to get more for your money the American way.

* $19,698 as shown in photograph

+ Use EST MPG for comparison. Mileage may vary depending on speed, trip length, and weather. Actual highway mileage lower.

A. Circle the letter in front of the phrase that correctly completes each sentence.

1. The Pashubi ad stresses that
   a. the gas mileage of the 630-X is comparable to that of other cars.
   b. the 630-X is designed with the driver in mind.
   c. you get more for your money when you buy the Pashubi.

2. The Tilton ad stresses that
   a. much of the Star's standard equipment is considered extra on other cars.
   b. the Star uses fewer robot welds than any other compact car.
   c. you get more for your money when you buy a Star.

3. All car ads must state the estimated miles per gallon (EST MPG) of gas that a car needs for highway (HWY) and for city driving. So a car boasting 43 EST HWY MPG, 28 EST MPG means that
   a. its estimated mileage is 43 miles per gallon for highway driving and 28 for city driving.
   b. its estimated mileage is 28 miles per gallon for highway driving and 43 for city driving.
   c. its actual mileage is 43 miles per gallon for highway driving and 28 for city driving.

4. Both ads advise that the gas mileage may vary from the estimates because
   a. the gas mileage the cars get probably has never been tested.
   b. the cars probably get much better mileage than the ad states.
   c. the cars may get lower gas mileage than the ad states.

5. The ad states that the Star is sold for as low as $16,999, but the car pictured in the ad costs $19,698. The price of the car in the picture is probably higher because
   a. it has many of the extra features, such as two-tone paint and a luggage rack.
   b. it is not really a Star but another kind of car made by Tilton.
   c. $16,999 is the sale price.

6. The standard equipment common to both the 630-X and the Star includes
   a. a leather-covered steering wheel and two-tone paint.
   b. power disc brakes and CD player.
   c. an electrically heated outside rearview mirror and power windows.

B. Complete the chart comparing the 630-X and the Star. If no information is given for a particular item, write NI. Then answer each question.

	630-X	STAR
Price	$20,025	$16,999
Number of passengers	4	6
City gas mileage	28 EST MPG	26 EST MPG
Number of standard equipment features	30	3
Country where the car is made	NI	U.S.

1. Which car do you think is made in Japan? _____

2. Which car comes with more standard equipment? _____

3. Which car holds more people? _____

Lesson 43 _____

Character

Reading a Literature Selection

▶ Background Information

Long ago, many Native American boys tested and proved their bravery in battle and by counting coup. To count coup, a warrior would approach his enemy and touch him with a coup stick. He would not kill him. Those days, are now gone. And Native American boys must show their bravery in other ways.

In "Test of Fire," Tom Swift Eagle, a young Lakota Sioux, grew up in a city where he had to find a way to prove his bravery. In this story, Tom faces a test as difficult as any that his ancestors ever faced.

▶ Skill Focus

The people in a story are called **characters**. Some stories have many characters. Others have only one or two. A story usually has only one **main character**. The other characters are not as important as the main character.

The main character usually wants to reach a goal or solve a problem. Look for the main character's actions and the reasons for them. These actions and their causes tell you the kind of person the main character is.

When you read a story, keep in mind the questions below. They will help you understand the main character.

1. Who is the main character?
2. What goal does the main character want to reach? Why is it important for the main character to reach this goal?
3. What problem does the main character want to solve? Why is it important for the main character to solve this problem?
4. What kind of person is the main character at the beginning of the story?
5. How does the main character change by the end of the story?
6. What has the main character learned by the end of the story?

▶ Word Clues

Read the sentences that follow. Look for context clues that explain the underlined word.

Some of the Native Americans Tom grew up with no longer followed the old traditions. In Tom's family, however, these old customs were not forgotten.

If you do not know the meaning of the word *traditions,* the word *customs* in the next sentence can help you. The words *traditions* and *customs* are synonyms. Traditions are customs.

Use **synonym** context clues to find the meaning of the three underlined words in the selection.

▶ Strategy Tip

Tom is the main character in "Test of Fire." As you read, think about what Tom wants to do. His actions tell you a lot about the kind of person he is. Does he pass his "test of fire"? Does he change by the end of the story?

Test of Fire

Excitement ran through Tom Swift Eagle as he looked out the plane window. This would be his training unit's first jump with other firefighters.

These firefighters belonged to a special group called smoke jumpers. They were trained to jump from planes to fight fires in parts of a forest that could not be reached by firefighters on the ground. Tom thought smoke jumpers were the bravest men alive. Today he would have the chance to use all that John Dull Knife had taught him. He would show himself to be as brave as the bravest smoke jumper.

Long ago, every Lakota boy learned how to become a warrior. He learned the arts of shooting arrows, throwing spears, tracking animals, and fighting enemies. To become a man, a boy had to go through several sacred ceremonies. Once he became a man and received his adult name, he was expected to prove his bravery by counting coup and going on his first buffalo hunt.

Those days are gone now. Many Native Americans, like Tom and his family, live in cities. Some of the Native Americans Tom grew up with no longer followed the old traditions. In Tom's family, however, the old customs were not forgotten.

But Tom lived in the 1990s. He couldn't prove his bravery as his ancestors had done in the past. Instead of proving himself with a bow and arrow, he would show his bravery by fighting a forest fire.

Tom pressed his face to the plane window and watched the green woods below him. Then he saw it. Great clouds of thick, black smoke were foaming up into the sky. His heart beat faster and faster.

Others in the plane had fought fierce fires like this one many times before. They were talking together as they got their gear ready. Their equipment included hard hats, gloves, shovels, and axes.

"This fire is a bad one," Rita Connelly said gravely.

Bill Williams nodded. "Soon Pineville will be nothing but ashes unless we can stop the fire," he said.

The test that Tom faced today was far more important than any test at school. He had to pass this test. It was a test of life or death.

Tom wanted nothing more than the respect of these brave firefighters. He reached inside his shirt to be sure that he was wearing his sacred medicine bag. The medicine bag contained sacred objects that would protect him. It was important to Tom to have his sacred medicine with him when he made his first jump.

It was almost time to jump. Jumping at the right instant was important. Smoke jumpers have to land near the fire without falling into the hungry flames.

At John's signal, Tom leaped out of the plane. He slowly dropped through the smoky air—down, down, toward the raging fire. He guided his parachute to an open spot between the trees. He had learned how to keep his parachute from getting hung up in tree branches.

As Tom hit the ground, the sharp smell of burning wood surrounded him. He heard the great fire roaring in the distance like a huge waterfall.

The firefighters quickly put on their hard hats and protective gloves. Armed with shovels and axes, they set to work making a firebreak. They cut down trees and cleared away brush on a wide strip of land in front of the racing flames. Then they scraped away some of the soil till bare ground showed. When the fire reached this bare ground, it would have nothing to feed on and would stop.

If they could finish in time.

The fire was moving fast, pushed by the wind and by its own heat. The air was full of flying sparks, ash, and falling branches.

Tom swung his ax as fast as he could. He could hardly breathe the hot, smoke-filled air. He had never felt anything like this heat. The thick smoke stung his eyes and burned his throat.

A crackling sound was all around them. The popping noises from dry, burning wood grew louder. Worst of all were the echoing booms as trees crashed down. Tom worked as he had never worked before.

Over the roar of the fire, Tom heard John shout, "Hurry! The fire is almost on us!"

Tom's arms were sore and tired, but he swung his ax even faster. He didn't even stop to wipe the tears from his stinging eyes. The greedy fire kept coming. The more the fire destroyed, the more it wanted. Tom worked shoulder to shoulder with the other smoke jumpers. His only thought was to stop the flaming monster that was raging through the forest.

At last the the smoke jumpers finished the firebreak. If the fire was powerful enough, it would jump over the firebreak that they had worked so hard to make. Then they would have to start all over again.

Tom stood motionless, his face black with ash, his shirt wet with sweat. He was too exhausted to move. He had given all of himself to fighting the fire. He turned his head and noticed John watching him. John nodded.

Suddenly all that John had taught Tom

> *A man is brave only when he forgets about himself.*

about proving his bravery was clear. A man was not brave if he did something just to prove his courage. He was brave only when he forgot about himself. Today Tom had showed that he cared very much about the others with whom he was working. Like John, Bill, Rita, and the others, he wanted most of all to stop the fire.

"Look!" Rita yelled.

The fire was burning down. It was not going to jump the firebreak.

"Pineville is saved!" Tom cried. He felt more tired than he ever had in his life. Yet a feeling of joy rose in Tom. He had proved that, like the other brave smoke jumpers, he could make a contribution. He had helped his friends save Pineville.

John put his hand on Tom's shoulder, as the others looked on. "Good work, Tom," he said. "Glad you're with us." Tom knew that he had passed his test and proven his bravery.

1. Why did the firefighters jump from planes instead of going to the fire in trucks?

   _____

2. Why is it important that the firefighters jump at just the right time?

   _____

   _____

   _____

3. What is in danger if the fire isn't stopped?

   _____

4. a. Where did Tom grow up?

   _____

   b. Where does Tom fight the fire?

   _____

5. Who prepared Tom for his "test of fire"?

   _____

6. What does Tom wear on his first jump?

   _____

7. Why does the fire stop when it reaches the firebreak?

   _____

   _____

8. What is the most exciting moment in the story's plot?

   _____

   _____

   _____

9. Draw a line to match each word to its correct meaning.

   gear   wanting more

   crackling   equipment for a
                   certain task

   greedy   bursting

INTERPRETING FACTS

1. At the beginning of the story, why does the test of fire mean more to Tom than any test at school?

   _____

   _____

2. What would the firefighters have to do if the fire jumped over the firebreak?

   _____

   _____

3. Do you think that Swift Eagle is an appropriate adult name for Tom? Tell why.

   _____

   _____

   _____

   _____

   _____

4. How does Tom Swift Eagle pass his "test of fire"?

_____

_____

5. Why does John say to Tom, "Glad you're with us"?

_____

_____

6. There is a message in "Test of Fire." What do you think the author is trying to tell you?

_____

_____

_____

SKILL FOCUS

Understanding the main character's actions will help you appreciate the story.

1. Who is the main character?

_____

2. a. What goal does he want to reach?

_____

b. Why is it important for him to reach this goal?

_____

3. What kind of person is Tom at the beginning of the story?

_____

_____

4. How has Tom changed by the end of the story?

_____

_____

_____

5. What has Tom learned by the end of the story?

_____

_____

_____

▶ **Real Life Connections** Describe someone who you think is brave.

Primary Source

___ Reading a Social Studies Selection___

▶ **Background Information**

The Nez Percé lived in the plateau country, an area that is now where the states of Washington, Oregon, and Idaho meet. The Nez Percé originally called themselves Nee Me Poo, which means "the Real People." French-Canadian fur trappers called them Nez Percé and the people adopted the name, pronouncing it *nez purse.*

The most famous chief of the Nez Percé was Chief Joseph, whose Indian name was Thunder Traveling to Loftier Mountain Heights. Joseph was 31 years old when he became chief after the death of his father.

In this lesson, you will read about Chief Joseph. You will also read the stirring speech that he delivered to President Hayes in Washington, D.C.

▶ **Skill Focus**

Using a **primary source** will help you learn about past events. A primary source is a firsthand account. It is usually written by a person who took part in the event being described. Primary sources give facts about events. They also give insight into the thoughts and feelings of the

people in the events. Letters, speeches, and newspaper articles are primary sources.

Often textbooks, magazines, encyclopedias, and so on, will contain excerpts, or pieces, of primary source materials. These excerpts are usually set apart in some way from the rest of the text.

When reading a primary source, use the following two steps.

1. **Find out all you can about the primary source.** Ask yourself the following questions.
   a. What type of document is it? Is it a letter, a report, an article, or a speech?
   b. Who wrote it? Was the author part of the event?
   c. When was it written?
2. **Study the primary source to learn about a past event.** Try to distinguish facts from opinions. A fact can be proven. An opinion is a judgment that reflects a person's feelings or beliefs.
   a. What facts can I learn from this document?
   b. What was the author's opinion about what was reported?

▶ **Word Clues**

Read the sentences below. Look for context clues that explain the underlined word.

As the early settlers moved west, they came into conflict with the Indians who lived there. The settlers had left their homes to find new land. They wanted land for farming and for raising cattle.

If you do not know the word *settlers* in the first sentence, read the next two sentences. They give details about the settlers. The details tell more about the word so that you understand it.

Use **detail** context clues to find the meaning of the three underlined words in the selection.

▶ **Strategy Tip**

As you read Chief Joseph's words, keep in mind the two steps for using a primary source. Reading this speech will give you insight into the thoughts and feelings of Chief Joseph and his people.

A Great and Honorable Leader

The Gold Rush

The Nez Percé lived peacefully in their country for hundreds of years. They had experienced good relations with the white trappers and explorers. But in 1860, white prospectors illegally entered Nez Percé territory and found gold. During the gold rush, thousands of miners settled on Nez Percé reservation lands, disobeying an earlier treaty. For the first time, friction developed between whites and the Nez Percé.

In 1863, under pressure from the gold miners to remove the Nez Percé from valuable mineral sources, the U.S. government demanded that the Nez Percé cede, or give up, about 6 million acres of reservation land. The majority of Nez Percé refused. A government commissioner bribed several chiefs who sold the land and signed the treaty. The government official reported to the U.S. government that he had secured all lands demanded "at a cost not exceeding 8 cents per acre."

As a result of the land sale, the Nez Percé divided into "treaty" and "nontreaty" bands. Among those who were angry about the selling of Indian land was Tuekakas, also known as Old Joseph. By 1871, thousands of settlers had moved onto reservation land, as was allowed by the new treaty. Near his death, Old Joseph spoke to his son Young Joseph about their homeland:

> *My son, my body is returning to my mother earth, and my spirit is going very soon to see the Great Spirit Chief. When I am gone, think of your country. You are the chief of these people. They look to you to guide them. Always remember that your father never sold his country. You must stop your ears whenever you are asked to sign a treaty selling your home.*
>
> *. . . My son, never forget my dying words. This country holds your father's body. Never sell the bones of your father and your mother.*

Chief of Peace

Upon his father's death, Joseph became the civil, or peace, chief of his father's band. Joseph held many councils, or meetings, with civil and military officials. In 1873, Joseph convinced the government that it had not legally secured title to the reservation lands. The government ordered the whites to move out of the territory. However, the government then reversed its decision under pressure from Oregon politicians and settlers.

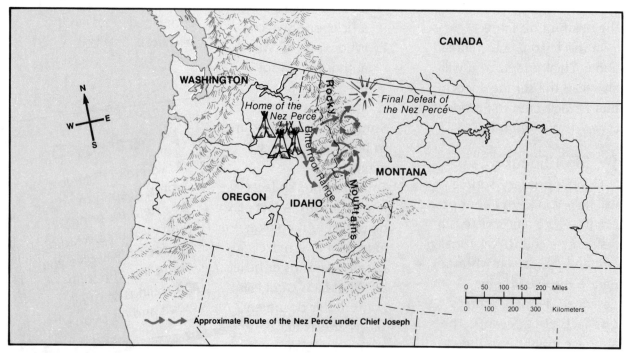

This map shows the retreat of the Nez Percé.

Understanding the dilemma of the U.S. government, Joseph continued to strive for a peaceful solution to the land problem. In 1877, General Oliver O. Howard concluded that the only solution was to force all the Nez Percé off their land and onto a reservation in Washington.

Many of the "nontreaty" Nez Percé wanted to fight for their land. Chief Joseph didn't want to fight. He knew that fighting would only bring death and sadness to his people. Joseph believed that he had no other choice but to lead his people to the reservation. So in the spring of 1877, Joseph agreed to the demands of the U.S. government. Several other nontreaty bands joined Joseph's for one last gathering on their land. While there, several men decided to seek revenge on white settlers for the death of one's father and for other grievances. They killed four white settlers.

Knowing that General Howard would send troops after them, the bands withdrew to White Bird Canyon. Thus began a remarkable <u>retreat</u>, in which the Nez Percé fought, alluded, and outwitted one military force after another for four months. With about 750 people, including sick and elderly people, women, and children, the Nez Percé circled over a thousand miles trying to reach safety in Canada.

The soldiers who fought Chief Joseph thought that he was a great and honorable man. The soldiers knew that the Nez Percé never killed without reason. They could have burned and destroyed the property of many settlers, but they did not. Joseph and his people fought only to defend themselves and their land. The white soldiers were also impressed with their ability to elude the army for so many months and over so many miles.

"I Will Fight No More, Forever"

But the end finally came. Unaware that the army under Colonel Nelson A. Miles was in close <u>pursuit</u>, the Nez Percé camped less than 40 miles south of the Canadian border. At the end of a five-day siege, Chief Joseph decided to <u>surrender</u> to Miles on October 5, 1877. He rode into the army camp alone and handed his rifle to the soldiers. He said:

I am tired of fighting. My people ask me for food and I have none to give. It is cold and we have no blankets, no wood. My people are starving. . . . Hear me, my chiefs. I have fought, but from where the sun now stands, Joseph will fight no more, forever.

After Joseph's surrender, the U.S. government ordered them onto a reservation in Kansas, then to a disease-ridden reservation in Oklahoma. Many of the Nez Percé died of malaria and other sicknesses.

Chief Joseph pleaded on behalf of his people to gain permission to return to a reservation in the Northwest. In 1879, Chief Joseph traveled to Washington to plead his case to President Hayes.

Chief Joseph's Speech

If the white man wants to live in peace with the Indian, he can live in peace. There need be no trouble. Treat all men alike. Give them the same laws. Give them all an even chance to live and grow.

All men are made by the same Great Spirit Chief. They are all brothers. The earth is the mother of all people, and all people should have equal rights upon it. You might as well expect all rivers to run backward as that any man born a free man should be contented penned up and denied liberty to go where he pleases. If you tie a horse to a stake, do you expect he will grow fat? If you pen an Indian

Chief Joseph of the Nez Percé Indians.

up on a small spot of earth and compel him to stay there, he will not be contented, nor will he grow and prosper.

I have asked some of the Great White Chiefs where they get their authority to say to the Indian that he shall stay in one place, while he sees white men going where they please. They cannot tell me.

I only ask of the government to be treated as all other men are treated. If I cannot go to my own home, let me have a home in a country where my people will not die so fast. I would like to go to Bitterroot Valley. There my people would be healthy; where they are now, they are dying. . . . Three have died since I left my camp to come to Washington. When I think of our condition, my heart is heavy. I see men of my own race treated as outlaws and driven from country to country, or shot down like animals.

Whenever the white man treats the Indian as they treat each other, then we shall have no more wars. We shall all be alike—brothers of one father and mother, with one sky above us and one country around us and one government for all. Then the Great Spirit Chief who rules above will smile upon this land and send rain to wash out the bloody spots made by brothers' hands upon the face of the earth. For this time, the Indian race are waiting and praying. I hope no more groans of wounded men and women will ever go to the ear of the Great Spirit Chief above, and that all people may be one people.

In 1885, after eight years of campaigning on behalf of his people, Joseph and the other Nez Percé were allowed to return to the Northwest. Unable to join the treaty bands on the Idaho reservation, Joseph and the others were escorted to the Colville Reservation in Washington Territory. It was there that Joseph died in 1904, reportedly from a broken heart.

RECALLING FACTS

1. Where did the Nez Percé originally live?

_____

_____

2. Why did the settlers want the Nez Percé land?

_____

_____

3. What event divided the Nez Percé into two groups

_____

_____

_____

4. Why did Chief Joseph lead his people to the reservation in 1877?

_____

_____

_____

5. Why did the soldiers think that Chief Joseph was a great leader?

_____

_____

_____

_____

6. After living on a reservation, where did Chief Joseph say he wanted to take his people? Why?

_____

_____

_____

7. Write the letter of the correct meaning in front of each word.

_____ retreat   a. following in order to capture

_____ pursuit   b. to give up

_____ surrender   c. to go to a safe place

1. For each pair of sentences, circle the letter next to the statement that expresses Chief Joseph's thoughts and opinions in his speech.

   a. The white man can live in peace with the Indian if all men are treated alike under the same law.

   b. Because so many promises have been broken, there can never be peace between the white man and the Indian.

   a. There will be no more wars when the settlers sign a peace treaty with the Indians.

   b. There will be no more wars when the settlers treat the Indians as they treat each other.

2. Decide whether Chief Joseph is a great and honorable leader. To reach a conclusion, you must look carefully at Chief Joseph's actions and the reasons for them. His major actions are listed in order below. For each action Chief Joseph takes, give the reasons.

   a. Chief Joseph first agrees to lead his people to the reservation without a fight.

   _____

   _____

   b. Chief Joseph decides to lead his people to Canada.

   _____

   _____

   _____

   c. Chief Joseph will fight the army only if they try to stop him.

   _____

   _____

   d. Chief Joseph leads his people on a twisting trail through the mountains for four months.

   _____

   _____

   e. During this time, Chief Joseph tries not to get into battles with the army.

   _____

   _____

   f. Chief Joseph says that he will "fight no more, forever" and leads his people to the reservation.

   _____

   _____

   _____

   g. Two years later, Chief Joseph speaks out against being "penned up" on a reservation even though he led his people there.

   _____

   _____

Now answer this question: Do you think that Chief Joseph was a great and honorable leader? In your answer, first tell what you mean by the words *great* and by *honorable*. Then tell why you think Chief Joseph was or was not a great and honorable leader.

_____

_____

_____

_____

_____

_____

_____

SKILL FOCUS

Reread Chief Joseph's speech. Pay special attention to what it tells you about Chief Joseph's feelings and motives. Then answer the questions below.

1. Find out all you can about the primary source.

What type of document is this? _____

Who wrote it? _____

Was the author involved in the event? _____

When was it written? _____

2. Study the primary source to learn about a past event.

What facts can you learn from this document? _____

_____

_____

_____

What was the author's opinion about what was reported? _____

_____

_____

_____

▶ **Real Life Connections** Write an interesting fact or story about the history of your community. List your primary sources.

Main Idea and Supporting Details

___ Reading a Science Selection _____

▶ Background Information

National parks and wilderness areas are areas set aside by the federal government for everyone to enjoy. Many of these areas remain undeveloped so that their natural beauty is unspoiled. However, because of lack of funding the future of these parks and wilderness areas is now threatened. In this selection, you will read about the ways in which some people are destroying these areas.

▶ Skill Focus

When reading textbooks, it is helpful to look for **main ideas and supporting details.** As you know, the main idea is the most important idea in a paragraph. The supporting details tell more about the main idea. They help to prove that the main idea is true.

Read the paragraph below.

> Sandra loves to ride horses. She saved the money that she earned after school to buy a horse. Now she rides her horse every day. She also goes roller-blading three times a week.

The first sentence has the main idea. It says that Sandra loves to ride horses. The second sentence says that she saved her money to buy a horse. This sentence supports the main idea because a person who does not love to ride horses probably wouldn't buy one. The third sentence also supports the main idea. However, the last sentence does not support the main idea. The fact that Sandra roller-blades three times a week has nothing to do with her love of horses. This sentence does not belong in the paragraph.

When you read a selection that is packed with information, use the following steps:

1. Find the main idea in each paragraph.
2. Find the supporting details that tell about this main idea.
3. Reread the supporting details carefully and decide whether they support the main idea.

▶ Word Clues

Read the following sentences. Look for detail clues that explain the underlined word.

> Today's national parks are the result of work done long ago. Beautiful trees and ponds have been handed down to us by people who cared about nature. The efforts to save some of our natural <u>heritage</u> began more than one hundred years ago.

The word *heritage* in the last sentence is explained by the sentences before it. These sentences give details about our natural heritage. They help you understand the meaning of the word *heritage.*

Use **detail** context clues to find the meaning of the three underlined words in the selection.

> ### ▶ Strategy Tip
>
> As you read each paragraph in the following selection, try to find the supporting details for each main idea. Remember that each paragraph has one main idea, which can be stated in any sentence in the paragraph.

Preserving Park and Wilderness Areas

1. For years, people have been changing the earth, but the changes have not always been for the better. Suddenly, we discover that the best scenery and wilderness areas are disappearing. Every summer, millions of people take outdoor vacations in hope of enjoying nature. Too often they find parks crowded with people, fast food restaurants, and gift shops.

2. Today's national parks are the result of work done long ago. Beautiful trees and ponds have been handed down to us by people who cared about nature. The efforts to save our natural heritage began more than one hundred years ago. In 1872, the U.S. Congress passed a law setting up Yellowstone National Park for public use. Since then, about two hundred other national park areas have been set up. They are run by the National Park Service. Hundreds of state parks have also been set up. Many parks are overcrowded in the summer. Over the years, more and more people are visiting national parks

3. Because of <u>vandalism</u>, federal and state governments are finding it difficult to keep up the parks. It is difficult to believe that there are people who like to destroy or spoil beautiful things. Unfortunately, some people ruin things and places that everyone could enjoy. Some people damage museum <u>exhibits</u>. Objects, such as valuable paintings, jewels, or old books and clothing, are displayed in museums. There is always the chance that these artifacts will be damaged. Some people throw all kinds of litter in park areas. Others spoil what is left of very old buildings by writing on them. They use paint or lipstick that makes cleaning and repairing difficult to do. The <u>defacement</u> of historic buildings and monuments has become a big problem. Millions of dollars are spent each year to repair damage caused by vandals.

4. Not everybody understands how important **sanctuaries** (SANK chew wer eez) and wilderness areas are. Sanctuaries are places where it is illegal to hunt birds and animals. Many people do not seem to understand why roads should not be built through these areas. They don't see why homes and businesses are not allowed in them. If these places were built up with homes and roads, they couldn't be used for **habitat** (HAB ə tat) studies. A habitat is an area where a certain type of animal is usually found.

5. Some ranchers would like to raise more cattle. Some mining companies would like to dig for minerals. Some real estate developers would like to build houses and sell land in "undeveloped" areas. Some people who are very eager to make more money don't want more public parks.

1. When did Congress set up Yellowstone National Park as a public park?

   _____

2. Why are national and state governments finding it difficult to keep up the parks?

   _____

3. What is a wildlife sanctuary?

   _____

   _____

4. What do some mining companies want to do in undeveloped areas?

   _____

INTERPRETING FACTS

1. Why might the building of roads and homes in wildlife sanctuaries ruin habitat studies?

   _____

   _____

2. How do wilderness areas disappear?

   _____

   _____

   _____

3. Decide if each of the following statements is true or false. Write *true* or *false* on the lines.

   a. Picking up trash on the sidewalk would be considered vandalism.

   _____

   b. A display of movie costumes and a showcase of puppets are both exhibits.

   _____

   c. Sticking chewing gum on the seat of a bus is an example of defacement.

   _____

SKILL FOCUS

The main idea of each numbered paragraph is given below. Write the supporting details on the lines below each main idea. Use your own words. Leave out any details that do not support the main idea. The first one is done for you.

Paragraph 1

Main Idea   For many years, people have been changing the earth, but the changes have not always been for the better.

Supporting Details

   a. Much of the best wilderness land is disappearing.

   b. Millions of people take outdoor vacations in the hope of enjoying nature.

   c. Parks and wilderness areas are crowded with people, restaurants, and shops.

Paragraph 2

Main Idea   The efforts to save our natural heritage began more than one hundred years ago.

Supporting Details

a. _____

b. _____

c. _____

d. _____

Paragraph 3

Main Idea   Because of vandalism, federal and state governments are finding it difficult to keep up the parks.

Supporting Details

a. _____

b. _____

c. _____

d. _____

e. _____

f. _____

Paragraph 4

Main Idea   Not everybody understands that sanctuaries and wilderness areas are important.

Supporting Details

a. _____

b. _____

c. _____

Paragraph 5

Main Idea   Some people who are very eager to make more money don't want more public parks.

Supporting Details

a. _____

b. _____

c. _____

▶ **Real Life Connections** What could you do to beautify or preserve a park or wilderness area in your city or town?

Reading a Table

Reading a Mathematics Selection

▶ Background Information

As you probably already know, organization is an important skill to learn. When you are organized, you will usually succeed at whatever task you are doing.

When you look at a table, think about what is really happening. The numbers are *organized* so that the person looking at the table can gather the information that he or she needs in a short period of time.

In this way, tables are really nothing more than tools for your convenience. Just like a calculator or a ruler, tables are there to assist you.

Imagine for a moment that you live in a world without tables. Because there are no tables, you would probably use lists to present most information. One of the drawbacks with lists is that the information is not as readily available. It would probably take you twice as long to find the information that you need.

In the following lesson, you will learn about the growth in population as settlers moved west from 1790 to 1830. In addition, you will learn how easy it is to use and read tables, as well as how to set up a table from information presented in a paragraph.

When reading the following selection, remember to read the table carefully. Read across the rows and then down the columns. Notice the headings.

▶ Skill Focus

Information can be presented in a variety of ways, such as tables, charts, and diagrams. It is a valuable skill to be able to read and interpret information that is presented in these ways.

Tables that show number facts appear in many books, including textbooks, encyclopedias magazines, and newspapers.

You read tables to find certain facts, as well as to compare facts. It is often easier to find and use number facts presented in a table than number facts given in a paragraph. When reading a table, first read the title and the headings. They will tell you what the numbers in the table stand for.

▶ Word Clues

Look for the following words in the selection: *population, data, asterisk.* Be sure that you understand their meanings.

Use **synonym** context clues to find the meaning of these words if you are unfamiliar with the words. Remember that synonym clues use familiar words to restate and, therefore, define the unfamiliar words. Synonym clues can often be found in the same sentence. They can also be found in the sentence before or the sentence after the sentence in which the unfamiliar word appears.

▶ Strategy Tip

When reading a mathematics selection, you must learn how to read information that is presented in tables, charts, and diagrams.

In order to get all the information from a table, remember to read both across the rows and down the columns.

Reading a Table

Shortly after Europeans came to the New World, they established 13 colonies in what are now Maine, New Hampshire, Rhode Island, Massachusetts, Connecticut, New York, New Jersey, Pennsylvania, Maryland, Virginia, North Carolina, South Carolina, and Georgia. Over time, though, people began to look toward the West. Slowly at first, brave individuals and families loaded everything that they owned into wagons and moved West. When gold was discovered in California in 1849, the westward migration increased rapidly. Populations in other areas increased again during the gold rushes of 1860 and 1874.

The table below presents information on the populations of several states during the years 1790–1830. Population means "the number of people living in an area." These states were among the first ones to be colonized in the West after the first 13 colonies in the East. Information, or data, about population is often shown in a table.

The title of the table tells what the table shows. Always read the title before studying a table. In the chart below, the states are listed in the column on the far left. The years are printed across the top. The population figures are listed in columns under each year.

✔ When reading a table, you may wish to use a sheet of paper or ruler to make sure that you are looking at the correct row. Place a sheet of paper under the word *Indiana* in the chart. Now look across until you find the number in the column labeled 1830. The number is 343,000. This number means that there were 343,000 people living in Indiana in 1830.

Read across from *Kentucky*. You can see that in the year 1790, there were 73,600 people living in Kentucky. In the year 1800, 221,000 people were living there. Keep reading across and find Kentucky's population in 1810, 1820, and 1830. As you can see, the number of people living in Kentucky increased over the years.

Now look down the column on the far left until you find Illinois. Did the number of people living in Illinois also increase over the years?

Look for Michigan's population in 1800. The star, or asterisk, in that column tells you to look at the bottom of the table. In the lower left corner of the table, find the words *no data available*. In other words, there is no record of the population of Michigan in the year 1800.

Population Growth in the West 1790–1830					
	1790	1800	1810	1820	1830
Alabama	*	1,250	9,050	127,900	309,500
Arkansas	*	*	1,060	14,300	30,400
Illinois	*	*	12,300	55,200	157,400
Indiana	*	5,600	24,500	148,200	343,000
Kentucky	73,600	221,000	406,500	564,300	687,900
Louisiana	*	*	76,600	153,400	215,700
Michigan	*	*	4,760	8,900	31,400
Mississippi	*	7,600	31,300	75,400	136,600
Missouri	*	*	19,800	66,600	140,500
Ohio	*	45,400	230,800	581,400	937,900
Tennessee	35,690	105,600	261,700	422,800	681,900

*no data available

Use the table on page 134 to answer the following questions.

1. Which state had the largest population in 1820? _____

2. Which state had the smallest population in 1800? _____

3. For Missouri, what does the asterisk mean under 1790? _____

4. From 1810 to 1820, did the population of Ohio or Kentucky increase more? _____

5. Which state had the lowest population in 1830? _____

6. What should you read first before studying a table? _____

7. When reading a table, what should you use to make sure that you are looking at the correct

   row? _____

8. Reread the paragraph that has a check mark next to it. Draw a line under the sentence that has the main idea.

INTERPRETING FACTS

Use the table on page 134 to answer the following questions.

1. Why are the states listed in the table in alphabetical order?

   _____

   _____

   _____

2. Why do you think there is more information available in later years than in early years?

   _____

   _____

   _____

3. Why might the population of the western states have increased faster than the population in northeastern states?

   _____

   _____

   _____

A. Use the table below to answer the questions that follow.

Native American Population by Selected Regions, 1990	
Region	**Population**
Northeastern States	33,000
Mountain States	481,000
Pacific States	362,000
South Atlantic States	156,000

1. What is the title of the table?

_____

_____

2. What is the Native American population of the Mountain States region?

_____

_____

3. Which region has a Native American population of 362,000?

_____

4. Which region has the largest Native American population?

_____

5. What is the total Native American population in the Northeastern States and Mountain States?

_____

6. What is the difference between the population of Native Americans in the Pacific States region and those in the South Atlantic States region?

_____

B. Use the information in the following paragraph to complete the table below. The paragraph gives information about some federal and state reservations for Native Americans.

Arizona has 23 reservations where 203,500 Native Americans live. Massachusetts has only 1 reservation, with 12,200 people living there. New York has 8 reservations for 62,700 people. Wyoming has 1 reservation where 9,500 people live.

Some Federal and State Reservations for Native Americans		
State	**Number of Reservations**	**Population**
Arizona		
Massachusetts		
New York		
Wyoming		

C. Make your own table using the following information. Then write three questions about your table. Use another sheet of paper for your table and questions.

In 1990, there were 203,500 Native Americans in Arizona. Oklahoma had about 252,400 Native Americans, and South Dakota had 50,600. Washington state had 81,500 Native Americans. Minnesota had 50,000.

▶ **Real Life Connections** Create a table showing the population growth of your community or state over the last 10 years.

Syllables

You have used three guides for dividing words into **syllables**: Guide 1, dividing between the two smaller words in a compound word; Guide 2, dividing between double consonants; and Guide 3, dividing between a prefix or suffix and a root word. Now you will have practice in using another guide.

Words with Two Consonants Between Two Sounded Vowels

The words in the list below have been divided into syllables. Write an answer to each of the questions in the headings below.

	How many sounded vowels?	*How many consonants between the vowels?*	*Where is the word divided?*
dan ger	_____	_____	_____
bas ket	_____	_____	_____
mar ket	_____	_____	_____
har bor	_____	_____	_____
don key	_____	_____	_____
pic ture	_____	_____	_____

Fill in the words necessary to complete the following guide.

Guide 4: A word that has two _____ between two sounded _____ is usually divided into syllables between the two _____ .

Divide each word below into two syllables by writing each syllable separately on the line to the right of the word.

1. winter _____
2. turban _____
3. number _____
4. shelter _____
5. jersey _____
6. larva _____

7. magnet _____
8. seldom _____
9. practice _____
10. circus _____
11. hemlock _____
12. surface _____

13. sentence _____
14. monkey _____
15. furnace _____
16. service _____
17. entire _____
18. compare _____

Syllables

Words with One Consonant Between Two Sounded Vowels

Here is a guide that will help you divide words into **syllables**. It shows you how to divide words that have one consonant between two sounded vowels. The guide has two parts.

The words in the list below are divided into syllables. Write an answer to each of the questions in the headings.

	How many sounded vowels?	How many consonants between the vowels?	Is the first vowel long or short?	Is the word divided before or after the consonant?
spi der	_____	_____	_____	_____
me ter	_____	_____	_____	_____
to tal	_____	_____	_____	_____

Fill in the words necessary to complete the first guide.

Guide 5a: A word that has one _____ between two sounded _____,

with the first vowel long, is usually divided into syllables before the _____.

Divide each of the words below into two syllables by writing each syllable separately on the line to the right of the word.

1. tiger _____   **3.** pilot_____   **5.** silent _____

2. local_____   **4.** moment_____   **6.** minus_____

To complete the second part of the guide, write an answer to each of the questions in the headings below.

	How many sounded vowels?	How many consonants between the vowels?	Is the first vowel long or short?	Is the word divided before or after the consonant?
cab in	_____	_____	_____	_____
top ic	_____	_____	_____	_____
riv er	_____	_____	_____	_____

Fill in the words necessary to complete the second guide.

Guide 5b: A word that has one _____ between two sounded vowels, with the first

_____ _____, is usually divided into syllables _____ the _____.

Words with Blends

The word *betray* has two consonants between the two sounded vowels, but you do not divide the word between the two consonants.

bet ray

Since *tr* is a consonant blend, it is considered in the same way that one consonant would be considered. So Guide 5a applies, and the word is divided before the blend.

be tray

If three consonants are in the middle of a word, it is possible that two of those consonants are a blend. You treat the blend as one consonant. For example, *compress* has a *pr* blend. You divide the word between the consonant and the consonant blend.

com press

In words ending with a consonant and *-le,* these letter groups are treated as one syllable.

tum ble

Circle the blend or consonant and *-le,* in each word below. Then divide the word into syllables by writing each syllable separately on the line to the right of the word.

1. replied _____

2. congress _____

3. declare_____

4. children _____

5. explain _____

6. control_____

7. increase _____

8. complain _____

9. purple _____

10. subtract_____

11. cradle_____

12. matron_____

13. central _____

14. reply_____

15. secret _____

16. supply _____

17. curdle_____

18. substance_____

19. complete _____

20. stable_____

21. Pilgrim_____

22. microbe_____

23. muscle_____

24. hustle_____

25. tremble _____

26. between_____

27. circle _____

28. emblem _____

29. comprise _____

30. paddle _____

Fill in the words necessary to complete the following guide.

Guide 6: Do not split a consonant _____ or a consonant and _____.
Treat a consonant blend or _____ and *-le* as if it were one consonant.

Making Inferences

In many of the paragraphs that you read, information is given about a subject. You can use this information to **infer** other information. When you infer, you put together what you read in the selection with what you already know about a topic to figure out something new.

Read the following selection about Ada Deer. Answer the questions by making inferences about what you read.

Ada E. Deer was born and raised in a one-room log cabin on the Menominee Indian Reservation in Wisconsin. All during her childhood, Ada Deer believed that education was very important. When she was ready for college, her tribe gave her a scholarship. She became the first Menominee to graduate from the University of Wisconsin. Later, she was the first Native American to obtain a master's degree in social work from Columbia University in New York City.

Deer's education included law school, but in the 1970s she dropped out to help her people. The Menominee were

struggling for survival. Their land, once held in trust for them by the government, had lost its trust status. She wrote: "As a teenager, I saw the poverty of the people—poor housing, poor education, poor health. I thought, this isn't the way it should be. . . . I wanted to help the tribe in some way. . . . "

Ada Deer became a tribal chief and a social worker. In helping Native Americans, she has kept her vow to repay her tribe for giving her a chance for a higher education. As of 1995, she was working for the U.S. government at the Bureau of Indian Affairs as its assistant secretary.

1. Why do you think that Ada Deer's tribe gave her a scholarship?

_____

_____

2. How do you know Ada Deer works hard?

_____

_____

3. How did Ada Deer repay her tribe for making higher education possible?

_____

4. How do you think Ada Deer feels about Native Americans?

_____

5. How do you think Ada Deer would feel about the ability of people to change things?

_____

Alphabetical Order

Below are some words that you might find in a science textbook. These words are not in **alphabetical order.** On the numbered lines, write the words in alphabetical order according to the first letter in each word. Cross out each word in the list after you write it.

kerosene	tide	1. _____	13. _____
nectar	lake	2. _____	14. _____
underground	jet	3. _____	15. _____
equator	bees	4. _____	16. _____
planet	ocean	5. _____	17. _____
Venus	star	6. _____	18. _____
quartz	wind	7. _____	19. _____
fish	cell	8. _____	20. _____
hail	moon	9. _____	21. _____
dew	X-ray	10. _____	22. _____
insect	ant	11. _____	23. _____
root	germ	12. _____	24. _____

In a dictionary, you see many pages of words that begin with the same letter. What if you are looking up a word that begins with letter *p*? To find the word, turn to the *p* section of the dictionary, and use the second letter of the word as a guide. For example, the word *pattern* is listed before the word *platter* because *a* comes before *l* in the alphabet. When several words begin with the same letter, they are arranged in alphabetical order according to the second letter in the word.

Below are some words that you might find in a social studies textbook. On the numbered lines, write the words in alphabetical order according to the first two letters in each word. Cross out each word in the list after you write it.

arctic	atlas	1. _____	8. _____
age	aviation	2. _____	9. _____
Asia	Africa	3. _____	10. _____
axis	automobile	4. _____	11. _____
alfalfa	Andes	5. _____	12. _____
airplanes	Aztec	6. _____	13. _____
adobe	Amazon	7. _____	14. _____

Lesson 51

Guide Words

At the top of each dictionary page are two words by themselves. These words are called **guide words.** Guide words help you find entry words easily and quickly. They tell you the first entry word on the page and the last entry word on the page. All the other entry words on that page come between these two words in alphabetical order.

Below are two pairs of guide words that might appear on two dictionary pages. Following each pair is a list of entry words. If an entry word would be on the same page as the guide words, write *yes* next to the word. If an entry word would appear on an earlier page, write *before.* If an entry word would appear on a later page, write *after.* Some of the entry words in each list begin with the same first two letters. You will need to look at the third letters to complete this activity.

pencil/polite

1. percent _____
2. pouch _____
3. pepper _____
4. pay _____
5. pearl _____
6. power _____
7. permit _____
8. pigeon _____

9. pool _____
10. pebble _____
11. petunia _____
12. pocket _____
13. pelican _____
14. point _____
15. pony _____
16. poet _____

17. pedal _____
18. porcupine _____
19. pester _____
20. play _____
21. patient _____
22. perch _____
23. polish _____
24. poodle _____

gem/goose

1. gear _____
2. geography _____
3. graduate _____
4. giant _____
5. gown _____
6. golf _____
7. gather _____
8. gelatin _____

9. general _____
10. goggle _____
11. got _____
12. geranium _____
13. geese _____
14. goat _____
15. gently _____
16. govern _____

17. gone _____
18. gourd _____
19. gaze _____
20. gift _____
21. good _____
22. genius _____
23. gate _____
24. gorilla _____

Dictionary Entry

In a dictionary, the entry word and all the information about it is the **entry**. The entry word always appears in boldface type. If the word has more than one syllable, it is divided into syllables to show where the word can be divided at the end of a line of writing.

The entry word is followed by a **respelling** of the word in parentheses. The respelling shows you how to pronounce the word.

The part-of-speech label follows the respelling. The labels are usually abbreviated as follows: *adj.* for adjective, *adv.* for adverb, *conj.* for conjunction, *interj.* for interjection, *n.* for noun, *prep.* for preposition, *pron.* for pronoun, and *v.* for verb.

The meanings are arranged according to parts of speech. For example, if an entry has noun meanings, they are grouped together and numbered following the *n.* label. Any meanings the word may have for other parts of speech are numbered and placed after the appropriate labels. When an entry has only one meaning for any part of speech, the definition is not numbered.

At the end of some entries are phrases or idioms. An **idiom** is a group of words that has a meaning different from the meaning the words have by themselves. In some dictionaries, idioms have a dash in front of them and appear in boldface type.

Use the dictionary entry below to answer the questions that follow it.

> **wear** (wer) *v.* **1** to have or carry on the body [*Wear* your coat. Do you *wear* glasses?] **2** to have or show in the way one appears [She *wore* a frown. He *wears* his hair long.] **3** to make or become damaged, used up, etc., by use or friction [She *wore* her jeans to rags. The water is *wearing* away the river bank.] **4** to make by use or friction [He *wore* a hole in his sock.] **5** to last in use [This cloth *wears* well.] **6** to pass gradually [The year *wore* on.]—**wore, worn, wear′ing** ◆*n.* **1** the act of wearing or the condition of being worn [a dress for holiday *wear.*] **2** clothes; clothing [men's *wear*]. **3** the damage or loss from use or friction [These shoes show a little *wear.*] **4** the ability to last in use [There's a lot of *wear* left in that tire.]—**wear down, 1** to become less in height or thickness by use or friction. **2** to overcome by continuing to try [to *wear down* an enemy].—**wear off,** to pass away gradually [The effects of the medicine *wore off.*]—**wear out, 1** to make or become useless from much use or friction. **2** to tire out; exhaust.

1. What is the entry word? _____

2. Write the respelling. _____

3. How many verb meanings follow the part-of-speech label *v.*? _____

4. How many noun meanings follow the part-of-speech label *n.*? _____

5. Write the first noun meaning. _____

6. What is the fifth verb meaning? _____

7. Write the idiom with the same meaning as the underlined words below.

   Jane <u>overcame by continuous effort</u> her dad's resistance to buying her a car. _____

   A full day at the amusement park was enough to <u>tire out</u> Jill. _____

Library Catalog

To locate a book in the library quickly and easily, use the **library catalog.** In most cases, the catalog will be a computer database. You find the information that you want by choosing items from a menu or list. On the main, or first menu, one of the numbered items will be the library catalog. When you choose that item, a second menu will appear. Now you can choose to search for a book by the title, author's name, or subject that it is about. If you don't have exact information about the book, you may be able to choose an item called **key words.** The computer will search its database using only one or two important words that you give it.

The catalog gives more information than just the author, title, and subject of a book. Usually each entry gives a summary and describes the book (size, number of pages, kinds of illustrations). It also gives the publisher, the date of publication, and a list of related subjects. It may also tell how many copies there are, which libraries have the book, and whether it is available.

Suppose you want a book about space flight. First, you choose "Subject" from the catalog menu to do a **subject search.** Then you enter the words *space flight.* (You could also enter words such as *space exploration, outer space,* or *astronauts.*) A list of subjects will appear. Choose your subject to see a list of books about that topic. Then you can choose a particular book to find out more about it.

If you want to find a list of books written by a particular author that are in the library, you can do an **author search.** Choose "Author" from the catalog menu and enter the author's name, last name first (for example: Vogt, Gregory). A list of authors will appear. Choose your author to see a list of his or her books. You can then choose a particular book to find out more about it.

If you already know what book you want, you can do a **title search.** Choose "Title" from the catalog menu and enter the exact title. An alphabetical list of titles will appear, including the one you entered. If the title begins with *A, An,* or *The,* the book will be listed by the second word in the title. You can then select the title of the book that you want.

In each kind of search, the last step is to choose a particular book. When you do, a screen like this one will appear:

```
Call Number            Children's Nonfiction          Status: in
J629.4  VOGT 1991

AUTHOR                 Vogt, Gregory
TITLE                  Voyager
SERIES                 Missions in space
PUBLISHER              Brookfield, Connecticut: Millbrook Press,
                       c. 1991
DESCRIPTION            111 pages; color ill.; 24 cm.
SUMMARY                Important new scientific data was collected on the planets
                       Jupiter, Saturn, Neptune, and Pluto by the telescopes aboard
                       the Voyager spacecrafts. For the first time, scientists
                       were able to collect information by studying the giant
                       planets at close range.

SUBJECTS               Space flight; Interplanetary voyages; Planets;
                       Outer space — Exploration
```

Notice the call number at the top of the screen on page 144. This number appears on the spine, or narrow back edge, of the book. Every nonfiction book has its own call number that tells where it is shelved in the library. Nonfiction books are kept in numerical order. The *J* stands for *juvenile*. It tells you that this book is for young readers. Across from the call number is the word *status*. This tells you whether the book is on the shelf or is checked out.

A. Now use the screen to do the following.

1. This book is one of several books in a series. Underline the name of the series.

2. How new is the information in this book? Circle the year that the book was published.

3. What kind of pictures does this book have? Put two lines under the information that tells you.

4. The subject used for this search was *space flight*. Draw a box around other subjects that you could use in your search.

B. Circle the kind of search that you would do to answer each question.

1. Who wrote the book *Animals in Orbit: Monkeynauts and Other Pioneers in Space?*

    author search   title search   subject search

2. Does the library have any books about smoke jumpers?

    author search   title search   subject search

3. What books by Roberto Terpilauskas are in the library?

    author search   title search   subject search

C. Use the information on the screen below to answer each question.

```
Call Number          Children's Nonfiction      Status: checked in
J629.45409 RIDE

AUTHOR               Ride, Sally
TITLE                To space and back
PUBLISHER            New York: Lothrop, Lee & Shepard, c. 1986
DESCRIPTION          96 pages; color ill.; 29 cm.
SUMMARY              Describes in text and photographs what it is like to
                     be an astronaut on the space shuttle Challenger.
                     Includes a glossary of terms.
SUBJECTS             Space flight; Space shuttles
```

1. Suppose you want to find other books by this author. What name would you look under?

    _____

2. Will this book most likely tell you all about how astronauts are trained? _____

3. Suppose you want to know more about the space shuttle program. What subject could you

    search under? _____

4. What is the call number of this book? _____

Lesson 54

Using a Bus Route Map

Suppose you want to visit a friend who is in the hospital. It is too far from your home to walk, so you decide to take a bus. But it is the first time that you have had to take a bus, and you have no idea which bus to take. What should you do? Your local bus company, perhaps called the Transit Authority, prints a map showing bus routes. Bus routes are the ways different buses travel in your city. Using a **route map,** you can find the best way to travel by bus from place to place.

Examine the bus route map below. The map shows some of the main streets in a city. Different bus routes are indicated on the map. The key below the map will help you read and understand the bus route.

A. Read each statement about the bus route map. Fill in the circle before **true** or **false**.

1. Six bus routes are shown on the map.

     ○ true   ○ false

2. Buses on route 6 travel on Hill Street.

     ○ true   ○ false

3. Buses on route 6 run north and south.

     ○ true   ○ false

4. Buses on route 2 travel in two directions.

     ○ true   ○ false

5. Buses on route 8 run north and south on Second Street and west on Parkview Avenue.

    ○ true   ○ false

6. Buses on route 6 travel 24 hours a day.

    ○ true   ○ false

7. Buses on routes 6 and 8 travel past Gillian Park.

    ○ true   ○ false

8. Buses on route 2 travel east on Mulligan Avenue.

    ○ true   ○ false

9. Going south, bus route 8 runs south on Gillian Street, east on Mulligan Avenue, and south again on Second Street.

    ○ true   ○ false

10. Buses on routes 8 travel on four different streets.

    ○ true   ○ false

11. Buses on routes 6 and 8 travel past Riverside Park.

    ○ true   ○ false

12. You can travel from Gillian Park to City Hall without changing buses.

    ○ true   ○ false

13. To go from the corner of Hill Street and River Road to the corner of Mulligan Avenue and Layton Street, you must take three buses.

    ○ true   ○ false

14. You cannot go on one bus from the corner of Gillian Street and Russell Road to the corner of Mulligan Avenue and Hill Street.

    ○ true   ○ false

B. Use the route map to answer each question.

1. Rachel lives at the corner of Kensington Terrace and Mulligan Avenue. She wants to go to the library. Which bus routes should she use?

_____

_____

2. Timothy and his sisters are at the movie theater on the corner of Parkview Avenue and Hill Street. Which bus route can they take to go to Riverside Park? _____

3. How can Dr. Chin get to City Hall from the Medical Center?

_____

_____

4. Marvin wants to go from Nevens Street and Parkview to the Forsyth Museum. What is the closest bus route? _____ What route can he use to return home? _____

5. What two ways could Rosa travel from Strawtown School to Jake's Pet Store?

_____

_____

6. How can Mr. Goldman get from Master Street near River Road to the Fix-it Repair Shop?

_____

_____

Scene, Dialogue, Stage Directions

Reading a Literature Selection

▶ **Background Information**

This play is based on a folktale set in ancient Ghana, in western Africa. It is about a trickster named Anansi. A trickster is a humorous character who uses pranks to outwit others. Anansi meets his match, however, when he thinks that he has "tricked" Anene into helping him set his fish traps.

▶ **Skill Focus**

Like a short story, a play can have characters, plot, conflict, setting, and theme. A play, however, is different in form from a short story.

A play often has many parts. Each part is called a **scene**. When the time or place changes, the scene changes. The time and place are called the **setting** of the play. Information about the setting is usually found at the beginning of each scene. Sometimes much time has passed between one scene and another. The playwright, or author, may tell you at the beginning of the new scene what took place in between.

The characters in the play speak their lines. Their speeches are called **dialogue.** The name of the character who is speaking appears before the lines to be spoken.

When you read a play, you will often find instructions about how the actors are to use their voices or act out their roles. These notes from the author are called **stage directions.** They appear in italic type and are usually in parentheses.

As you read a play, follow these steps.
1. At the beginning of each **scene**, read any notes that describe the play's setting.
2. Note who is speaking each line of **dialogue.**
3. Read all the **stage directions.**

▶ **Word Clues**

When you read a selection, you may find words that you don't know. Read the following stage direction.

Anene walks to the left, toward Osansa, who is standing near the <u>wing</u>.

You can tell from the context clues that the *wings* are in a theater. However, there are no context clues to tell you where in a theater the wings are located. You will need to use a dictionary.

When you read an unknown word and there are not enough context clues to explain it, use a dictionary to find the word's meaning. You may find it more convenient to finish what you are reading first and then look up the word.

Use a **dictionary** to find the meaning of the three underlined words in the play.

▶ **Strategy Tip**

As you read "Anansi's Fishing Expedition," notice who is speaking in each scene and how the setting changes. Pay attention to the notes at the beginning of each scene. Also, read the stage directions carefully.

Anansi's Fishing Expedition

Cast

Anansi, a clever trickster
Osansa } friends tired of Anansi's tricks
Anene
Village Chief
Villagers

Scene One

The setting of this play is a west African village in a long-ago time. The action takes place along the banks of a river near the village. The river bank is at stage left, toward the rear of the stage. A grove of palm trees is at the far right rear of the stage. The village street runs along the front of the stage from left to right.

The action begins at center stage, where Anansi is sitting on the ground. Osansa approaches along the street.

Anansi: Hello there, friend Osansa. I have an idea. Why don't we go set our fish traps together? Then we shall sell our fish and be quite rich!

Osansa: No, Anansi. I have as much food as I can eat or sell. I am rich enough. Why don't you set your fish traps by yourself?

Anansi: Ha! Fish alone? Then I'd have to do all the work! What I need is a fool for a partner!

Osansa *(walks off to the left):* Well, I won't be your fool, but perhaps you'll find someone else.

Anene *(approaches from the right):* Good day, Anansi. What clever plans have you today?

Anansi: I am looking for someone to set fish traps with me tomorrow. We shall sell the fish and be quite rich.

Anene: That sounds like a fine idea. Two people can catch more fish than one. Yes, I'll do it.

Anansi: Good. Meet me in the palm grove at dawn.

Anene walks to the left, toward Osansa, who is standing near the wings.

Osansa: Don't you know he is trying to make a fool of you? He says he needs a fool to go fishing with him. He just wants someone to set the fish traps and do all the work while he gets all the money for the fish!

Anene: Don't worry, friend. I won't be Anansi's fool!

Scene Two

Early the next morning, Anene and Anansi meet in the palm grove near the village.

Anene: Give me the knife, Anansi. I shall cut the branches for the traps. We are partners. We share everything. My part of the work will be to cut the branches. Your part will be to get tired for me.

Anansi: Just a minute. Let me think. Why should I be the one to get tired?

Anene: Well, when there's work to be done, someone must get tired. So if I cut the branches, the least you can do is get tired for me.

Anansi: Ha! You take me for a fool? Give me the knife. I shall cut the branches, and you shall get tired for me!

Anansi takes the knife and begins the hard work of cutting branches. As he cuts, Anene, who is relaxing on the ground, groans loudly with weariness. When all the wood is cut, Anansi ties it in bundles.

Anene: Anansi, let me carry the wood, and you get tired for me.

Anansi: Oh no, my friend. I am not that simple-minded. I'll carry the wood myself, and you can take the weariness for me.

Anansi hoists the bundle to the top of his head, and the two set off toward the village,

walking center stage, then right, toward the wings.

Anene *(arrives at the village)*: Let me make the fish traps, Anansi, and you sit down and get tired for me.

Anansi: Oh no. You just keep on as you are.

Anansi makes the traps while Anene sits under a tree and groans with weariness.

Anansi *(to himself)*: Look at him there, moaning with weariness, practically dying from tiredness. All I have to do is the work! How silly he is!

Anene: Now that the traps are finished, Anansi, let me carry them to the water. Surely you won't mind getting a little tired for me.

Anansi: Oh no. You just come along and do your share. I'll carry the traps, and you get tired.

Anansi and Anene go to the river bank.

Anene *(at the water's edge)*: Now wait a minute, Anansi. Let's think a minute here.

There are sharks in the water. Someone is apt to get hurt. So let me go in and set the traps, and should a shark bite me, you can die for me.

Anansi: What do you take me for? I'll go in the water and set the traps. If I am bitten, you can die for me!

After the traps are set, Anansi and Anene walk back to the village.

Scene Three

The next morning, Anene and Anansi meet at the river's edge.

Anene: Anansi, there are only four fish in the traps. You take them. Tomorrow there will probably be more, and I'll take my turn.

Anansi: Now what do you take me for? Do you think I am that simple? Oh no, Anene. You take the four fish, and I'll take my turn tomorrow.

Anene takes the four fish to the village and sells them.

Scene Four

The next morning, Anene and Anansi meet again at the river's edge.

Anene: Anansi, take these sixteen fish. Little ones, too. I'll take my turn tomorrow.

Anansi: Of course you'll take your turn tomorrow, it's my turn today. *(stops to think)* Well now, you are trying to make a fool of me again! You want me to take these sixteen miserable little fish so that you can get the big catch tomorrow, don't you? Well, it's a good thing I'm alert! You take the sixteen today, and I'll take the big catch tomorrow.

Anene carries the sixteen fish to the market and sells them. The next day he again tricks Anansi into waiting one more day for a bigger catch.

Scene Five

On the sixth day, Anansi and Anene come to the traps and find them rotten, although they hold a very fine catch.

Anene: Well, it's certainly your turn today. I'm very glad of that. Look, the fish traps are rotten and worn out. We can't use them anymore. I'll tell you what; you take the fish to town and sell them. I'll take the rotten fish traps and sell them. The fish traps will bring an excellent price. What a wonderful idea!

Anansi: Just a moment. Don't be in such a hurry. I'll take the fish traps and sell them myself. If there's such a good price to be had, why shouldn't I get it? Oh no, you take the fish, my friend!

Anansi hoists the rotten fish traps on his head, and Anene carries the fish. They go to the village.

Anene *(walking through the streets and shouting)*: Fresh fish for sale! Fresh fish!

Villagers *(gather around Anene)*: Fresh fish! Wonderful! We'll buy some!

Anansi: Rotten fish traps! I have rotten fish traps for sale!

The villagers avoid Anansi.

Village Chief *(approaches Anansi)*: Now what do you take us for? Do you think we are <u>ignorant</u> people? Your friend Anene came and sold good fish, which the people want. But you come trying to sell something that isn't good for anything. You are smelling up the village with your rotten fish traps. You insult us. For this you must clean the homes of the people of the village. *(to the villagers)* Take him away.

Anansi is hauled offstage. Soon his moans are heard. He stumbles back onstage.

Anene: Anansi, this should be a lesson to you. You wanted a fool to take fishing. You didn't have far to look to find one. The fool you took fishing was you!

Anansi *(rubs his back and legs, which are tired from all the work he has done)*: Yes. But what kind of partner are you? *(looks <u>reproachfully</u> at Anene)* At least you could have taken the pain while I did all the cleaning!

1. Why doesn't Anansi want to set his own fish traps?

_____

2. Is Osansa fooled by Anansi's trick?

_____

_____

3. Whom does Anansi think he's tricked into setting his fish traps?

_____

_____

4. What four tasks must be performed to trap fish?

_____

_____

_____

5. While Anansi is making the fish traps, what is Anene doing?

_____

_____

_____

6. What tasks does Anene trick Anansi into doing?

_____

_____

7. Why is the village chief angry with Anansi for trying to sell the rotten fish traps?

_____

_____

_____

8. Why does Anansi have to clean the homes of the villagers?

_____

_____

9. Whom does Anansi really fool?

_____

10. Write the letter of the correct meaning in front of each word.

—— hoists   **a.** finding fault with

—— ignorant   **b.** lifts up

—— reproachfully   **c.** having little knowledge

INTERPRETING FACTS

1. Why do you think Osansa was not fooled by Anansi?

_____

_____

2. Do you think that Anene would have been fooled by Anansi if Osansa had not warned him? Explain.

_____

_____

_____

3. Who do you think is the cleverest character in the play? Explain.

_____

_____

4. Was Anansi trying to trick people by selling rotten fish traps? Explain.

_____

_____

5. Do you think Anansi deserved his punishment? Explain.

_____

_____

6. Are Anansi and Anene true-to-life characters? Explain.

_____

_____

7. What is the message of this play? Put a check mark in front of the correct statement of theme.

_____ Tricking one's friends can be fun.

_____ Tricksters can fool people only for so long; eventually the tricksters themselves will be fooled.

_____ Trickery means fooling people into doing your work for you.

SKILL FOCUS

Scenes, dialogue, and stage directions make a play different from a short story. Recognizing and understanding this difference in form will make it easier for you to read a play. To answer these questions, go back to the play.

1. Scene

There are several events in the plot of this play. Briefly tell about the setting and the important events in each scene.

Scene One

Setting: _____

Event: _____

_____

Scene Two

Setting: _____

Event: _____

Scene Three

Setting: _____

Event: _____

_____

Scene Four

Setting: _____

Event: _____

Scene Five

Setting: _____

Event: _____

_____

2. Dialogue

Reread the dialogue between Anansi and Anene in Scene Five after Anansi cleaned the villagers' homes. From what Anansi says to Anene, what lesson has Anansi learned?

_____

_____

_____

3. Stage Directions

Stage directions are notes from the playwright that appear at the beginning of a scene. Sometimes directions appear within or after lines of dialogue. Answer these questions from the information given in the stage directions.

a. What is the setting of the play?

_____

b. If Scene One occurs on day one, on what day does Scene Three occur?

_____

c. On what day do Anansi and Anene discover that their traps are rotten?

_____

d. How do the villagers respond to Anansi when he tries to sell his rotten fish traps?

_____

e. In his last speech, why does Anansi look reproachfully at Anene?

_____

_____

▶ **Real Life Connections**   How is the moral of the play applicable to life today?

Reading a Map

___Reading a Social Studies Selection _____

▶ Background Information

The Congo River in Africa is one of the world's longest rivers. It flows through many different regions of Africa. Many other rivers flow into the Congo River on its dramatic journey across Zaire to the Atlantic Ocean.

The Congo River, like many of the other great rivers (the Nile, Amazon, and Mississippi rivers) is very important to the people who live in the region. These people are often called river people. This name is given to these people because of their dependence on the river. Without the river, many of these people couldn't survive.

Almost all of these people fish. It is difficult to fish at times because of the fast-flowing waters of the Congo. People also farm the regions closest to the river. They grow crops, such as cassava, yams, bananas, and other fruits and vegetables. Farming is also often very difficult because of constant flooding, which can sometimes destroy entire crops.

In the following selection, you will learn more about the history and importance of the Congo River.

▶ Skill Focus

Two types of maps— physical maps and political maps— are often found in textbooks. A **physical map** shows surface features, such as plains, plateaus, mountains, lakes, and rivers. These features are often shown by different colors or shades of one color. For example, blue may be used to show bodies of water. A **political map** shows the location and boundaries of a country or state, a capital city, and other important cities. When a map combines features of both types of maps, it is called a **physical/ political map.**

Most maps have a scale of distance. This scale is helpful in measuring distances between two points on the map. One inch on a map can stand for one mile or several hundred miles. Most map scales also show distance in meters. One centimeter can stand for one kilometer or several hundred kilometers.

Remember to read the map key very carefully. The key or legend explains the colors, symbols, and scale of distance on a particular map. Reading a map along with the text will give you more information than either one could provide alone.

▶ Word Clues

Read the sentence below. Look for context clues that explain the underlined word.

> From its source, or starting point, the river flows north across gently sloping country.

If you do not know the meaning of the word *source,* the phrase *starting point* can help you. A source is a starting point. The term *starting point* is an appositive phrase. An appositive phrase explains a word coming before it and is set off from the word by commas or dashes.

Use **appositive phrases** to find the meaning of the three underlined words in the selection.

▶ Strategy Tip

As you read "The Congo River," look at the physical/political maps. The first map shows the location of Zaire. The second map shows the path of the Congo River. Before you begin to read, study the map key.

The Congo River

The Congo River, the world's tenth longest river, is in west central Africa in the country named Zaire (zah IR). The Congo River is 2,716 miles (4,370 kilometers) long. It is Zaire's most important waterway.

The Course of the Congo River

The Congo begins in the southeastern corner of Zaire, more than 1,000 miles (1,600 kilometers) south of the equator. From its source, or starting point, it flows north across this gently sloping country. The Congo River grows stronger and wider as tributaries—smaller rivers—feed into it. At this point, it is called the Lualaba (loo a LAH ba) River.

> The Congo River crosses the equator not once, but twice.

The river soon crosses the equator, and at Stanley Falls it becomes the Congo River. It then plunges down a group of cataracts, or large waterfalls, curving west across northern Zaire. The river's long westerly arc takes it south across the equator again to Kinshasa (keen SHAH sah), the capital of Zaire. At Kinshasa, the Congo widens to form Stanley Pool. Then, for 215 miles (346 kilometers), the river rushes over seven cataracts below Kinshasa. At this point, the river is a roaring mass, throwing up waves five and ten feet high. At Kinshasa, all Congo River freight must be changed from boat to rail. This is done to bypass the miles of cataracts that make the river unnavigable below Kinshasa. By the time the river reaches Matadi (mah TAH dee), it has dropped hundreds of feet in elevation. Located about 90 miles upriver from the coast, Matadi is Zaire's only port that ocean ships can reach.

The stretch of difficult water between Kinshasa and Matadi prevents boats from sailing from the coast to inland cities. This difficulty was a major factor in preventing the exploration of the heart of Africa in the nineteenth century.

Finally, the mighty Congo River empties into the Atlantic Ocean. Every other African river has a delta—a triangle of sand and soil left at the mouth of a river—but the Congo has none. Its muddy waters rush far out into the South Atlantic. Over the years, the powerful river has cut an underwater canyon in the ocean's floor. This canyon is 4,000 feet (1,200 meters) deep and goes 100 miles (160 kilometers) out into the sea.

A Unique River

The Congo pours 1.5 million cubic feet (.042 million cubic meters) of water into the Atlantic Ocean every second. It carries more water than any other river except the Amazon in South America. No other major river crosses the equator once, let alone twice. No other major river flows in both the Northern and Southern hemispheres.

The Congo River Basin

The basin of the Congo River is more than 1,000 feet (300 meters) above the level of the sea. A river basin is the area drained by a river and its tributaries. The Congo River basin can be thought of as a large plateau. It is flat, open country that makes up more than one-tenth of the land surface of the African

This map shows where Zaire is located on the African continent.

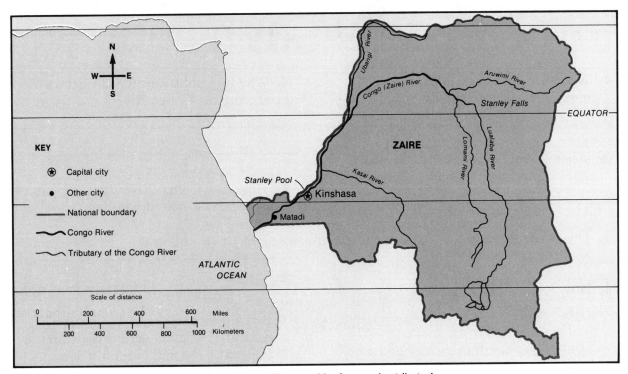

This map of Zaire shows the course of the Congo River and its four major tributaries.

continent. The Congo River basin includes all of Zaire and Congo, most of the Central African Republic, and parts of Zambia, Angola, Tanzania, and Cameroon. The area of the river basin is 1.5 million square miles (3.9 million square kilometers).

Tributaries of the Congo River

Many other rivers feed into the Congo River. The Congo has four major tributaries:

Even in the twentieth century, people and cargo are still transported along the Congo River in small dugout canoes.

the Ubangi (oo BAHN gee) and Aruwimi (ah roo WEE mee), two rivers that come into the Congo from the north; the Lomami (loh MAH mee) and Kasai (kah SY), both rivers from the south. These tributaries, together with the Congo, form a network of thousands of miles of navigable rivers throughout the Congo River basin.

The Discovery of the Congo River

Portuguese navigators were the first to locate the mouth of the Congo River. They found it ten years before Columbus landed in America. The Portuguese thought that the river would cut across Africa from the Atlantic Ocean to what they thought was the Indian Ocean. The cataracts a hundred miles upriver, however, kept them from further exploration. Nevertheless, they did find that the river was called *Nzadi*, or "big water," by the people. The Portuguese changed Nzadi to Zaire, which was easier for them to say. Years later, the river was given an African name, Congo. This name comes from the ancient Kingdom of Kongo that the Portuguese found when they arrived in 1482. After the Belgian Congo gained its independence in the 1960s, the country was renamed Zaire, and its mighty river became the Zaire River.

1. What was Zaire called before its independence in the 1960s?

_____

_____

2. What is Zaire's only port that ocean ships can reach?

_____

_____

3. The Congo River is the _____ longest river in the world.

4. How long is the Congo River?

_____

_____

5. How is the mouth of the Congo River unlike other African rivers?

_____

_____

6. Name two ways in which the Congo River is different from any other river.

_____

_____

_____

7. What are the four major rivers that feed the Congo?

_____

_____

8. Why was it difficult for navigators to explore the Congo River?

_____

_____

9. Why is all Congo River freight changed from boat to rail at Kinshasa?

_____

_____

_____

10. Reread the paragraph that has an **X** next to it. Then underline the sentence that states the main idea of the paragraph.

11. Underline the word that correctly completes each sentence.

   a. A triangle of sand and soil left at the mouth of a river is a _____.
   source   delta   course

   b. Smaller rivers that feed into a larger one are _____.
   waterways   cataracts   tributaries

   c. Large waterfalls are called _____.
   cataracts   tributaries   flows

1. What might be one reason that Kinshasa and not Matadi is the capital of Zaire?

_____

_____

_____

2. Why do you think that the Belgian Congo was renamed Zaire after its independence?

_____

_____

3. Look at the photograph on page 157. How are people and goods transported on the Congo River?

_____

Is this an efficient means of transportation? Explain.

_____

_____

4. You have already learned that the main idea is the most important idea in a paragraph. Sometimes you will be asked to figure out the main idea of a group of paragraphs or an entire selection. You can be sure that there will always be supporting details to tell about the main idea.

Only one of the following statements expresses the unstated main idea of the selection you just read. Circle the letter next to the statement that identifies the unstated main idea.

a. Four major tributaries feed into the Congo River.
b. The journey of the mighty Congo River makes it one of the world's most unusual rivers.
c. The Congo River is Zaire's most important waterway.
d. The Congo River is the sixth longest river in the world.

5. On the lines below, write at least five supporting details that tell about the main idea. You can go back to the selection to find the supporting details.

a. _____

b. _____

c. _____

d. _____

e. _____

SKILL FOCUS

Use the maps on pages 156 and 157 to answer the following questions. Be sure to reread the map key before you begin.

1. In what part of Africa is Zaire located?

_____

2. What is Zaire's capital city? How do you know?

_____

3. Name another important city in Zaire. How do you know it is a city?

_____

4. Locate the source of the Congo River. Circle it. Use it as the starting point to answer questions 5, 6, and 7.

5. Is the source of the Congo River north or south of the equator?

_____

6. From its source, in what direction does the Congo flow?

_____

7. Name the first tributary that flows into the Congo River.

_____

8. The Congo River basin is made up of the Congo River and all its tributaries. What color is this area on the first map?

_____

9. Put a check mark on the spot where the Congo River turns westward.

10. After the Ubangi River has joined the Congo River, in which direction does the Congo flow?

_____

11. Locate Stanley Pool. At this point, the Congo River has crossed the equator twice. Put an **X** on the map to mark each place.

12. Locate the mouth of the Congo River. Circle it. Into what body of water does the Congo River empty?

_____

13. Why would it be difficult to measure the length of the Congo River using the scale of miles?

_____

_____

_____

14. Based on the scale of distance, how far south of the equator is Matadi?

_____

15. Why is it more helpful to have two maps?

_____

_____

▶ **Real Life Connections** Use an encyclopedia or an atlas to find information about the longest river in the United States — the Mississippi. Compare information about the Mississippi River with what you have read about the Congo River.

Inferences

__ Reading a Science Selection __

▶ Background Information

Many different kinds of hoofed animals live in Africa. Most of these graze on the open plains. Other kinds of animals hunt them for food.

▶ Skill Focus

Sometimes you can **infer**, or figure out, information that is not stated directly in a selection.

Read the following paragraph. Try to infer the color of the bear's fur.

A polar bear will slowly crawl toward a sleeping seal. If the seal wakes up and raises its head to look around, the bear will stop moving and put its paw over its black nose. Then it is very difficult for the seal to see the bear against the snow.

The following clues can help you infer the color of the polar bear's fur: the bear covers its black nose with its paw; the bear is then difficult to see against the snow. So the bear becomes difficult to see only when its black nose is covered. You can infer that the bear is the same color as the snow—white.

You could infer several other facts from this

paragraph. You could infer that the bear doesn't want the seal to know that it is approaching. The following clues could help you figure this out: the seal is sleeping and when the seal looks around, the bear stops moving. You know that a sleeping animal would not see the bear coming toward it. The bear would be difficult to see when it is not moving. It would look like part of the snow. That is why the bear stops moving when the seal wakes up and looks around.

You could also infer that polar bears eat seals. You have already inferred that the polar bear doesn't want the seal to know that it is approaching. You know that some animals sneak up on other animals to kill them. If the seal saw the bear, the seal would jump into the water and escape.

If you go through the following steps, you will find it easier to infer information.

1. Read the selection carefully.
2. Think about what you've read. Be sure you understand the information that is stated in the selection.
3. Read again and look for clues to information not stated in the selection.

4. Put together the information stated in the selection with information that you already know. Use clues to help you make inferences.

▶ Word Clues

Read the sentences below. Look for context clues that explain the underlined word.

Some antelopes have <u>spiral</u> horns. *Spiral* means "turned or twisted."

If you do not know the meaning of the word *spiral,* read on. The second sentence states what the word *spiral* means. A word meaning that is stated directly can often be found before or after the new word.

Use **definition** context clues to find the meanings of the three underlined words in the selection.

▶ Strategy Tip

As you read the following selection on antelopes, pay close attention to all the facts. Use the facts to infer information that is not directly stated in the selection.

Antelopes

1. Antelopes are deerlike animals that live in the grassy plains of eastern and southern Africa and in parts of Asia. Like deer, antelopes are **herbivorous** (h ə r BIV ə r ə s) animals. They eat only grass, leaves, and fruit. All antelopes have two-toed hoofs and hollow horns. Some antelopes have spiral horns. *Spiral* means "turned or twisted." Others have straight horns. Antelope horns are different from a deer's antlers. A deer sheds its antlers every year and grows new ones. Antelopes have permanent horns. *Permanent* means "lasting for a long time."

✔ 2. There are over 150 different kinds of antelopes. Most of them live in Africa. Antelopes range in size from the large eland to the tiny dik-dik. The eland may stand up to 6 feet (1.8 meters) tall at the shoulder. It may weigh up to 1,500 pounds (680 kilograms). The dik-dik is about 2 feet long (61 centimeters), roughly the size of a jack rabbit.

> Q.: How is a deer different from an antelope?
> A.: An antelope never sheds its horns.

3. All antelopes are built for running. They use speed to get away from their enemies. They can usually outrun wild dogs, cheetahs, leopards, and lions. Antelopes can run at high speeds for a longer time than the big cats.

4. Gazelles and impalas are two of the fastest and most graceful of antelopes.

Gazelles are 2 to 3 feet (60 to 90 centimeters) tall at the shoulder. They can run as fast as 60 miles (96 kilometers) per hour for short distances. Impalas are about 3 feet (90 centimeters) tall at the shoulder. Impalas can cover 30 feet (9 meters) in one leap.

5. Antelopes are in the group called **ruminants** (ROO mə nənts). Ruminants include cattle, goats, deer, and giraffes. Most of these animals have horns and split hoofs. What makes ruminants different from other hoofed animals is that their stomachs have four <u>chambers</u>. A chamber is a closed space.

6. When a ruminant eats grass or leaves, it swallows without much chewing. The grass or leaves are then stored in the first chamber of the stomach. This chamber is called the **rumen** (ROO min). The grass or leaves slowly move to the second chamber. The second chamber is called the **reticulum** (re TIK yə ləm). In the reticulum, the grass or leaves are changed to a sticky substance called **cud**. When the animal is relaxed, the muscles of the reticulum send the cud back up to the mouth. The animal chews its cud thoroughly and swallows a second time. The cud passes through the rumen and the reticulum again and moves into a third chamber. The third chamber is called the **omasum** (oh MAY səm). From the omasum, the cud goes into the fourth chamber. This chamber is called the

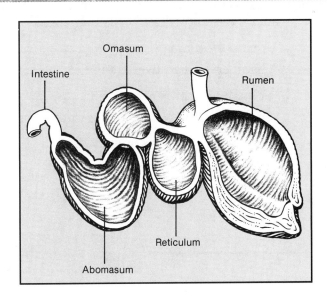

abomasum (ab ə MAY səm). In the abomasum, the cud mixes with <u>digestive</u> fluids and is completely broken down. *Digestion* means "helping to break down food so that it can be used by the body." The food then enters the small intestine, where it is sent into the animal's bloodstream.

7. Certain types of antelopes are now in danger of being wiped out. Cattle are grazed on more and more land that was once used by wild animals. Hunters kill antelopes for meat. However, laws are being passed to prevent antelopes from becoming extinct.

RECALLING FACTS

1. What do herbivorous animals eat?

_____

_____

2. What is the difference between a deer's antlers and an antelope's horns?

_____

_____

3. What is the largest type of antelope?

_____

_____

4. Why are all antelopes built for running?

_____

_____

5. On the diagram of a ruminant's stomach, put a check mark next to the chamber where the food is changed to cud. Put an X next to the chamber where the cud mixes with digestive fluids.

6. Reread the paragraph with a check mark next to it. Underline the sentence that has the main idea.

7. Underline the word or words that correctly complete each sentence.

   a. A closed-off area is a _____.
   chamber   digestive   tube

   b. Something that is permanent _____.
   changes often   lasts a long time   breaks easily

   c. Digestive juices help to _____.
   dissolve metal   break down food   burn oxygen

INTERPRETING FACTS

Circle the letter next to each correct answer.

1. Antelopes use their horns for _____.
   a. digging
   b. fighting
   c. running

2. A cheetah probably wouldn't hunt an eland because _____.
   a. elands are too strong for them
   b. elands are too fast for them
   c. elands are too difficult to see

3. Which of the following sentences states the main idea of Paragraph 6?
   a. Ruminants often have digestive problems because their stomachs have four chambers.
   b. Ruminants eat many different types of food.
   c. The digestive process of ruminants is quite complicated.

SKILL FOCUS

For each of the following statements, decide which of the items can be inferred from the paragraph listed. Put a check mark next to the statement or statements. On the lines that follow the three items, write the phrase or sentence that contains the clue that you found. Then explain how you inferred the information.

Paragraph 1 (check two)

_____ Most antelopes live in a warm climate.

_____ Most antelopes have long, slim legs.

_____ Most antelopes have pointed teeth.

Clue: _____

Explanation: _____

Clue: _____

Explanation: _____

_____

Paragraph 3 (check two)

_____ Some antelopes hide from their enemies.

_____ Antelopes must be very alert because they have many enemies.

_____ If a cheetah can't catch an antelope in the first few minutes of a chase, the antelope will escape.

Clue: _____

Explanation: _____

Clue: _____

Explanation: _____

_____

Paragraph 6 (check one)

_____ Ruminants must often eat quickly. They can't always take the time to chew their food because enemies might be nearby.

_____ Ruminants are larger than other hoofed animals.

_____ Ruminants prefer grass to leaves.

Clue: _____

Explanation: _____

_____

Paragraph 7 (check one)

_____ Cattle do not like antelopes.

_____ Africa is becoming more developed.

_____ Grazing cattle is against the law in Africa.

Clue: _____

Explanation: _____

_____

▶ **Real Life Connections** Investigate the current status of the antelope. Is it becoming an endangered animal? Support your response with facts.

Lesson 58

Reading Fractions

__ Reading a Mathematics Selection _____

▶ **Background Information**

Like other mathematical concepts, you use fractions everyday, probably without even realizing it. There are only so many instances in which everything can be depicted by whole numbers. Once you have an understanding of fractions, you will be able to do many more types of math problems.

You may recall reading about word problems in Unit 1. (See page 22.) You learned that you use word problems every day. The same can be said for fractions. In fact, you may even use fractions more than word problems. Let's look at a few examples in which you are thinking in terms of fractions without even realizing it.

In sports, statistics, or facts about a game, are recorded in terms of fractions. To determine whether a baseball player is a good batter, his or her batting average is recorded in terms of fractions. If a player gets a base hit seven out of every ten times that he or she is up to bat, then his or her

batting average for that game is $\frac{7}{10}$, or seven tenths.

Scores on tests are also figured out in terms of fractions. If you get 7 questions right out of a possible 12 questions, then your score is $\frac{7}{12}$, or seven twelfths.

Cooking is perhaps the most common way in which you use fractions. Many ingredients are measured in terms of $\frac{1}{2}$, $\frac{1}{4}$, or $\frac{1}{3}$ cups. These measurements are fractions of a whole cup in the same way that $\frac{1}{2}$ and $\frac{1}{4}$ teaspoons are fractions of a whole teaspoon.

As you read the following selection on fractions, try to picture what is being described. Look carefully at the diagrams. They show what the fractions stand for.

▶ **Skill Focus**

You use fractions every day. If an apple is cut into four equal parts and you eat three of them, you are eating a fraction of an apple. In a fraction, one number is written above a line and one is written below, like this:

$$\frac{3}{4}$$

You read these numbers together as *three fourths.*

▶ **Word Clues**

When you read a selection, you may find words that you don't understand. In this selection, there are two words that are important for you to learn and understand: *numerator* and *denominator.* Both of these words are defined in the selection. Be sure that you understand the meaning of both of these words.

▶ **Strategy Tip**

When reading a mathematics selection, it is important to read the text and look at the diagrams. Examine the diagrams carefully. They illustrate, or show, what the text is saying. Read the text and look at the diagrams several times, if necessary, until you understand what is being explained in the selection.

Reading Fractions

✔ A fraction shows a part of a whole. Suppose that you broke a stick into three equal parts. The fraction $\frac{1}{3}$ describes each part. You read this as *one-third*. If you have two of the parts, you have $\frac{2}{3}$ (two-thirds) of the whole stick. The fraction $\frac{2}{3}$ is larger than $\frac{1}{3}$. If you have $\frac{2}{3}$ of the stick, you have more parts of the whole than someone with $\frac{1}{3}$.

In the fraction $\frac{2}{3}$, the bottom number shows the number of parts into which the whole has been divided. It is called the **denominator**. The top number shows the number of parts that you have. It is called the **numerator**.

Figure 1

In Figure 1, the whole has been divided into three equal parts. Two of these parts are shaded. The fraction $\frac{2}{3}$ (two-thirds) can stand for the shaded parts of the whole.

Remember that in order to show fractions, the whole must first be divided into *equal* parts. Look at the diagrams in Figure 2. Into how many parts has each whole been divided?

| (a) | (b) | (c) |

Figure 2

Only one diagram, is divided into three *equal* parts. Only Figure 2(b) shows the fraction $\frac{1}{3}$ (one-third).

Look at Figure 3. The whole has been divided into how many equal parts? How many parts are shaded? What fraction shows how many of the parts are shaded?

Figure 3

The fraction $\frac{2}{6}$ (two-sixths) is correct.

Below are three more fractions. Study the diagrams and labels carefully.

(a)

$\frac{3}{12}$ (three-twelfths)

(b)

$\frac{2}{9}$ (two-ninths)

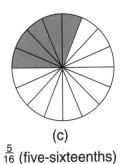

(c)

$\frac{5}{16}$ (five-sixteenths)

Figure 4

1. A fraction shows a —————— of a whole.

2. The bottom number in a fraction is called the ——————.

3. The top number in a fraction is called the ——————.

4. A fraction shows a whole divided into —————— parts.

5. The denominator shows —————— ——————.

6. The numerator shows —————— ——————.

7. Reread the paragraph that has a check mark next to it. Underline the sentence that has the main idea.

1. Put a check mark on the line next to the two situations in which you would have to use fractions.

—— **a.** when you go through the check-out counter at a grocery store

—— **b.** when you want to share a pie equally among several people

—— **c.** when you keep track of weekly attendance

—— **d.** when you are dividing property equally among four people

—— **e.** when you use public transportation

2. Tell about two recent situations in which you used fractions.

——————————————————————————

1. Look at the three diagrams below. In each diagram, a whole has been divided into equal parts. Write the fraction that stands for the shaded parts of the whole. Write your answer in the space next to each diagram.

a. ——————   a. ——————   a. ——————

2. A whole may be a single thing, or it may be a group of things. The following diagrams show two examples of a whole group divided into smaller, equal groups. Fill out the three columns for each example. In the last column, write the fraction that shows how many of the equal groups have been shaded. The first one has been done for you.

	Number of Equal Groups in Whole	Number of Groups Shaded	Fraction Shaded
a.	3	1	$\frac{1}{3}$
b.	_____	_____	_____

3. Shade in each diagram below to show the fraction next to it.

a. $\frac{4}{5}$	**e.** $\frac{1}{10}$
b. $\frac{1}{6}$	**f.** $\frac{1}{3}$
c. $\frac{2}{3}$	**g.** $\frac{2}{4}$
d. $\frac{4}{8}$	**h.** $\frac{3}{8}$

▶ **Real Life Connections** Tell about two recent situations in which you used fractions.

Lesson 59

Multiple Meanings

Sometimes words that we use every day have entirely different meanings when used in the context of science, geography, history, or mathematics. Some words with multiple meanings are listed below.

bank	cape	date	scale
bark	check	mouth	school
bed	crop	pole	yard

Read the two definitions for number 1. Choose a word from the list that goes with those two definitions. Write the word on the line. Do the rest of the lesson the same way.

1. _____

Common use: the opening in the head through which food is taken in
Geography: the place where a river empties into a larger body of water

2. _____

Common use: a written order to the bank to pay money to someone
Mathematics: to test the answers to problems to make sure that they are right

3. _____

Common use: a tall, slender piece of wood
Geography: the point farthest north or farthest south on the earth

4. _____

Common use: the fruit of one type of palm tree
History: the exact point in time at which an event takes place

5. _____

Common use: a piece of furniture on which to sleep
Geography: the bottom of a river

6. _____

Common use: the short, sharp noise made by dogs
Science: the outer covering of a tree

7. _____

Common use: the ground around or next to a house or other building
Mathematics: a measure of length

8. _____

Common use: a sleeveless garment worn around the shoulders
Geography: a piece of land extending into the water

9. _____

Common use: a place where money is deposited
Geography: land along the edge of a river

10. _____

Common use: a place for learning
Science: a large number of fish traveling in a group

11. _____

Common use: a weighing machine
Science: a small, flat, hard plate forming part of the covering of fishes and reptiles

12. _____

Common use: the yield of grain, fruit, or vegetables grown during one season
Science: a pouch in the throat of some birds

Prefixes

In your reading, you will frequently find a word that has a **prefix** added to the beginning of it. A prefix is a word part that changes the meaning of a word. Look at the following four prefixes and their meanings.

Prefix	Meaning
un	not
in	in, toward
re	back, again
pre	before

Write one of the listed prefixes on the line to the left of each word below. Make the new word mean the same thing as the phrase to the right of the word.

1. _____ fastened   not fastened

2. _____ check   to check again

3. _____ view   to view before

4. _____ land   toward the land

5. _____ appear   to appear again

6. _____ call   to call back

7. _____ covered   not covered

8. _____ view   to view again

9. _____ test   before the test

10. _____ pleasant   not pleasant

Below are some words to which prefixes have been added. Think about the meaning of the prefix before each word. Then write the meaning of the word.

1. uneven _____

2. remove _____

3. unable _____

4. unusual _____

5. income _____

6. repaint _____

7. preheat _____

8. redraw _____

9. unsafe _____

10. infield _____

11. preschool _____

12. prejudge _____

13. input _____

14. unbend _____

15. reread _____

16. prearrange _____

17. reclaim _____

18. rearrange _____

19. inshore _____

20. rejoin _____

21. unselfish _____

22. regain _____

Lesson 61

Suffixes

Many words have **suffixes** added to the ends of them. A suffix changes the meaning of the word. The meanings of five suffixes are given below. Suffixes often have several meanings. The most common meanings are given here.

Suffix	Meaning
er	one who does
en	made of, to become
ful	full of
ly	like in appearance or manner
ness	quality or state of

Write one of the listed suffixes on the line to the right of each root word below. Make the new word mean the same thing as the phrase to the right of the word.

1. wonder _____ full of wonder

2. hard _____ to become hard

3. quick _____ in a quick manner

4. dark _____ state of being dark

5. sing _____ one who sings

6. spoon _____ a full spoon

7. buy _____ one who buys

8. earth _____ made of earth

9. brother _____ like a brother

10. own _____ one who owns

Below are some root words to which suffixes have been added. Think about the meaning of the suffix at the end of each word. Then write the meaning of the word.

1. worker _____

2. queenly _____

3. thickness _____

4. sisterly _____

5. teacher _____

6. powerful _____

7. wooden _____

8. planter _____

9. fatherly _____

10. fighter _____

11. kindness _____

12. rancher _____

13. leader _____

14. friendly _____

15. darkness _____

16. strengthen _____

17. joyful _____

18. painter _____

19. quietly _____

20. loudness _____

Lesson 62

Encyclopedia

As you study science, social studies, and mathematics, you will frequently want to look up more information about a topic. Your best source for additional information is a set of books called an **encyclopedia.**

Look at the picture of an encyclopedia. The volumes are numbered in alphabetical order. Each volume has a letter or letters on its spine showing that topics beginning with that letter or letters are in that volume. Words beginning with *a* would be found in Volume 1; words beginning with *t, u,* and *v* would be found in Volume 14.

Use the picture of the encyclopedia to answer the following questions. Fill in the space between the lines to the left of the answer.

1. Ken looked at Volume 5. What do you think he was looking up?

   || butterflies

   || hippopotamus

   || elephants

2. Felipe wanted to look up reptiles. Which volume did he need?

   || 5 || 9 || 12

3. After he read about reptiles, Nick decided to look up crocodiles and snakes. Which two volumes did he use?

   || 3 and 13 || 3 and 10 || 14 and 3

4. Shannon had Volume 10. What might she have looked up?

   || parrots and plants

   || seals and snakes

   || mammals and moss

5. Tom wanted to find out all about dogs. What might he have looked up?

   || dogs, cats, and birds

   || dogs, pets, and mammals

   || dogs, reptiles, and snakes

6. Yuan had to do a report on salmon. Which volume did he need?

   || 6 || 11 || 13

7. At the end of the article on salmon, Jim found a note that read "*See fish.*" Which volume did he need next?

   || 3 || 6 || 8

8. Sue looked at Volume 14. What might she have looked up?

   || airplanes || tunnels || canals

9. Carla had to write a report on Meriwether Lewis and William Clark for social studies. Which two volumes did she need?

   || 4 and 9 || 9 and 3 || 3 and 12

10. Safar chose the explorer Robert LaSalle for his report. Which volume did he use?

    || 12 || 15 || 9

11. If Safar was using the volume that he needed for his report, would Carla have been able to do all her research?

    || yes || no

    Why? _____

Lesson 63

Using a Mall Floor Plan

You probably have visited a shopping center or mall. Some malls are quite large, with many stores. How can you find one particular store? Most malls have a **floor plan** that shows the location of all the stores in the mall. If you use the floor plan, you don't have to waste time walking up and down the mall looking for a certain store.

Examine the floor plan below. It shows where each store in the Randolph Road Shopping Mall is located. Look for the arrow (▲) on the floor plan. If you were looking at the floor plan in this mall, you would be standing at the place marked by the arrow. You would be able to find your way around the mall by using the floor plan.

The key below lists the stores in alphabetical order and indicates the number of the store on the floor plan. The key also explains what the symbols represent. Notice the numbers and the symbols on the floor plan. The numbers identify the stores in the mall. The symbols indicate other important places in the mall.

To locate a store, first find the name of the store in the alphabetical listing. Notice the numeral assigned to the store. Find that numeral on the floor plan.

Randolph Road Shopping Mall

10	Big 30 Bowling Lanes	**9**	Flowers by Kim	**15**	World of Beauty
14	Bon Voyage Travel Agency	**11**	Healthy Life Natural Foods	**6**	Ye Olde Popcorn Wagon
2	Books to Grow On	**8**	Holly Housewares		Bench
5	Cardon Computers	**12**	Nile Furniture Company		
13	Clothes Closet	**7**	Pretty Pets, Inc.		Public telephones
16	Dilly's Donuts	**1**	Rupert's Department Store		
4	Fancy Feet Shoes	**3**	Sports Scene		Restrooms

A. Use the floor plan to complete each sentence.

1. The store labeled 8 is _____.

2. The number _____ on the floor plan stands for Pretty Pets, Inc.

3. There are _____ public restrooms in the mall.

4. The store closest to the Big 30 Bowling Lanes is called _____.

5. If you park in Parking Lot 1, you would have to walk through _____ to get to Books to Grow On.

6. To go to the Big 30 Bowling Lanes, it is best to park in _____.

7. If you wanted to go to Cardon Computers, park in _____.

8. If you are tired of walking, you can sit down and rest on one of the _____ benches in the mall.

9. Between World of Beauty and Clothes Closet is _____.

10. The three ways to enter the mall include going through Rupert's Department Store, going through _____, and coming in the _____ Road entrance.

11. Walking from Books to Grow On to Cardon Computers, you pass _____ and _____.

12. The only restrooms in the mall are located next to _____.

B. Decide if each of the following questions can be answered using the mall's floor plan. Write *yes* or *no* on the lines.

1. Where can I get something to eat? ____

2. Does the pet shop sell parakeets? ____

3. On which side of the mall is the shoe store? ____

4. Is the mall open on Sundays? ____

5. Is the furniture store having a sale? ____

6. Where is the closest public telephone? ____

7. Where is the travel agency? ____

8. Is a jewelry store in the mall? ____

C. Use the floor plan to answer the following questions.

1. If you were leaving the mall through the Randolph Road exit and wanted to eat a snack on the way out, where would you stop?

_____

2. If you were shopping at World of Beauty and Books to Grow On, what would be the closest exit?

_____

_____

3. What is the name of one store located between Pretty Pets, Inc., and the Big 30 Bowling Lanes?

_____

4. Which two stores are on either side of the Clothes Closet?

_____

5. The restrooms are closest to which store?

_____

Context Clue Words

The following words are treated as context clue words in the lessons indicated. Lessons that provide instruction in a particular context clue type include an activity requiring students to use context clues to derive word meanings. Context clue words appear in the literature, social studies, and science selections and are underlined for ease of location.

Word	Lesson						
ambergris	2	density	15	harpoons	2	regulate	26
asterisk	46	digestive	57	helium	15	reproachfully	55
ballast	15	dirigible	15	heritage	45	retreat	44
barging	33	diseases	26	hoists	55	rotated	14
blubber	2	dock	14	ignorant	55	scallops	3
bustle	24	dunes	13	imports	34	settlers	44
cataracts	56	eased	33	intake stroke	35	source	56
chambers	57	efficient	34	interrupt	33	specific	26
charts	1	embarrassed	24	jolt	13	spermaceti	2
compression stroke	35	equine	25	joystick	14	spiral	57
consumer	34	exhaust stroke	35	legislate	34	substances	26
course	1	exhibits	45	livestock	25	surrender	44
crackling	43	flare	1	lobsters	3	traditions	43
crisp	24	flywheel	35	offerings	14	tributaries	56
crouching	33	galley	1	permanent	57	trudged	13
data	46	gear	43	population	46	urban	25
defacement	45	glared	13	portable	25	vandalism	45
delta	56	greedy	43	power stroke	35	vendors	24
		haddock	3	pursuit	44	wing	55

Concept Words

In lessons that feature social studies, science, or mathematics selections, words that are unique to the content and whose meanings are essential to the selection are treated as concept words. Many of these words appear in boldface type and are often followed by a phonetic respelling and a definition.

Word	Lesson						
abomasum	57	deci-	16	hydraulic	35	piston	35
airships	15	deciliter	16	kilo-	16	place holder	36
ascorbic acid	26	deficiency	26	kilogram	16	place value	36
bag	15	degrees	27	liter	16	pyridoxine	26
basket	15	denominator	58	meter	16	radiator	35
biotin	26	digit	36	milli-	16	reticulum	57
Celsius	27	explosion	35	milliliter	16	riboflavin	26
centi-	16	Fahrenheit	27	mollusks	3	rumen	57
centigrade	27	folic acid	26	neck	15	ruminants	57
crankshaft	35	gondola	15	niacin	26	sanctuaries	45
crustaceans	3	gram	16	numerator	58	synthetic	26
cud	57	habitat	45	nutrients	26	thiamin	26
cylinder	35	hecto-	16	omasum	57	valve	15
deca-	16	hectometer	16	organic	26	vertebrates	3
		herbivorous	57	pantothenic	26		